Working the Angles: The Shape of Pastoral Integrity is the second of three books on the work of pastors in North America. The three books together are designed to provide a biblical orientation and theological understanding in cultural conditions decidedly uncongenial to such orientation and understanding.

This second volume provides an antidote to the powerful pressures that reduce pastoral vocation to a managerial religious job of running a church by defining the distinctive work of the pastor as listening and helping others to listen to God as he speaks in Scripture, prayer, and the neighbor.

Five Smooth Stones for Pastoral Work is the first and *Under the Unpredictable Plant: An Exploration in Vocational Holiness* the third book in the series.

Eugene H. Peterson

Working the Angles

The Shape of Pastoral Integrity

WILLIAM B. EERDMANS PUBLISHING COMPANY
GRAND RAPIDS, MICHIGAN

Copyright © 1987 by Wm. B. Eerdmans Publishing Co.
255 Jefferson Ave. S.E., Grand Rapids, Michigan 49503
All rights reserved

New completely reset edition 1993

Printed in the United States of America

Reprinted 1996

Library of Congress Cataloging-in-Publication Data

Peterson, Eugene H., 1932-
Working the angles.
1. Pastoral Theology. I. Title.
BV4011.P44   1987   253'.2   87-5286

ISBN 0-8028-0265-6

For
Jeffrey Dirk Wilson

Contents

Contents

Third Angle
SPIRITUAL DIRECTION

Introduction

AMERICAN PASTORS are abandoning their posts, left and right, and at an alarming rate. They are not leaving their churches and getting other jobs. Congregations still pay their salaries. Their names remain on the church stationery and they continue to appear in pulpits on Sundays. But they are abandoning their posts, their *calling*. They have gone whoring after other gods. What they do with their time under the guise of pastoral ministry hasn't the remotest connection with what the church's pastors have done for most of twenty centuries.

A few of us are angry about it. We are angry because we have been deserted. Most of my colleagues who defined ministry for me, examined, ordained, and then installed me as a pastor in a congregation, a short while later walked off and left me, having, they said, more urgent things to do. The people I thought I would be working with disappeared when the work started. Being a pastor is difficult work; we want the companionship and counsel of allies. It is bitterly disappointing to enter a room full of people whom you have every reason to expect share the quest and commitments of pastoral work and find within ten minutes that they most definitely do not. They talk of images and statistics. They drop names. They discuss influence and status. Matters of God and the soul and Scripture are not grist for their mills.

The pastors of America have metamorphosed into a company of shopkeepers, and the shops they keep are churches. They are preoccupied with shopkeeper's concerns — how to keep the customers happy, how to lure customers away from competitors down the street, how to package the goods so that the customers will lay out more money.

Some of them are very good shopkeepers. They attract a lot of customers, pull in great sums of money, develop splendid reputations. Yet it is still shopkeeping; religious shopkeeping, to be sure, but shopkeeping all the same. The marketing strategies of the fast-food franchise occupy the waking minds of these entrepreneurs; while asleep they dream of the kind of success that will get the attention of journalists. "A walloping great congregation is fine, and fun," says Martin Thornton, "but what most communities really need is a couple of saints. The tragedy is that they may well be there in embryo, waiting to be discovered, waiting for sound training, waiting to be emancipated from the cult of the mediocre."[1]

The biblical fact is that there are no successful churches. There are, instead, communities of sinners, gathered before God week after week in towns and villages all over the world. The Holy Spirit gathers them and does his work in them. In these communities of sinners, one of the sinners is called pastor and given a designated responsibility in the community. The pastor's responsibility is to keep the community attentive to God. It is this responsibility that is being abandoned in spades.

---

1. Martin Thornton, *Spiritual Direction* (Boston: Cowley Publications, 1984), p. 27.

2

"Hot indignation seizes me . . ." (Ps. 119:53). I don't know how many share my anger. I know a few names. Altogether there can't be very many of us. Are there yet seven thousand who have not bowed the knee to Baal? Are there enough to be identifiable as a minority? I think so. We recognize each other from time to time. And much has been accomplished by minorities. And there must be any number of shopkeepers who by now are finding the pottage that they acquired in exchange for their ordination birthright pretty tasteless stuff and are growing wistful for a restoration to their calling. Is the wistfulness an ember strong enough to blaze into a fierce repudiation of their defection, allowing the word of God again to become fire in their mouths? Can my anger apply a bellows to those coals?

Three pastoral acts are so basic, so critical, that they determine the shape of everything else. The acts are praying, reading Scripture, and giving spiritual direction. Besides being basic, these three acts are quiet. They do not call attention to themselves and so are often not attended to. In the clamorous world of pastoral work nobody yells at us to engage in these acts. It is possible to do pastoral work to the satisfaction of the people who judge our competence and pay our salaries without being either diligent or skilled in them. Since almost never does anyone notice whether we do these things or not, and only occasionally does someone ask that we do them, these three acts of ministry suffer widespread neglect.

The three areas constitute acts of attention: prayer is an act in which I bring myself to attention before God; reading Scripture is an act of attending to God in his speech and action across two millennia in Israel and Christ; spiritual direction is

3

an act of giving attention to what God is doing in the person who happens to be before me at any given moment.

Always it is God to whom we are paying, or trying to pay, attention. The contexts, though, vary: in prayer the context is myself; in Scripture it is the community of faith in history; in spiritual direction it is the person before me. God is the one to whom we are being primarily attentive in these contexts, but it is never God-in-himself; rather, it is God-in-relationship — with me, with his people, with this person.

None of these acts is public, which means that no one knows for sure whether or not we are doing any of them. People hear us pray in worship, they listen to us preach and teach from the Scriptures, they notice when we are listening to them in a conversation, but they can never know if we are attending to *God* in any of this. It doesn't take many years in this business to realize that we can conduct a fairly respectable pastoral ministry without giving much more than ceremonial attention to God. Since we can omit these acts of attention without anybody noticing, and because each of the acts involves a great deal of rigor, it is easy and common to slight them.

This is not entirely our fault. Great crowds of people have entered into a grand conspiracy to eliminate prayer, Scripture, and spiritual direction from our lives. They are concerned with our image and standing, with what they can measure, with what produces successful church-building programs and impressive attendance charts, with sociological impact and economic viability. They do their best to fill our schedules with meetings and appointments so that there is time for neither solitude nor leisure to be before God, to ponder Scripture, to be unhurried with another person.

We get both ecclesiastical and community support in conducting a ministry that is inattentive to God and therefore without foundations. Still, that is no excuse. A professional, by some definitions, is someone who is committed to standards of integrity and performance that cannot be altered to suit people's tastes or what they are willing to pay for. Professionalism is in decline these days on all fronts — in medicine, in law, in politics, as well as among pastors — but it has not yet been repudiated. There are still a considerable number of professionals in all areas of life who do the hard work of staying true to what they were called to do, stubbornly refusing to do the easy work that the age asks of them.

I have found a metaphor from trigonometry to be useful in keeping this clear; I see these three essential acts of ministry as the angles of a triangle. Most of what we see in a triangle is lines. The lines come in various proportions to each other but what determines the proportions and the shape of the whole are the angles. The visible lines of pastoral work are preaching, teaching, and administration. The small angles of this ministry are prayer, Scripture, and spiritual direction. The length and proportions of the ministry "lines" are variable, fitting numerous circumstances and accommodating a wide range of pastoral gifts. If, though, the lines are disconnected from the angles and drawn willfully or at random, they no longer make a triangle. Pastoral work disconnected from the angle actions — the acts of attention to God in relation to myself, the biblical communities of Israel and church, the other person — is no longer given its shape by God. [Working the angles is what gives shape and integrity to the daily work of pastors and priests.] If we get the angles right it is a simple matter to draw in the lines. But if we are careless with or dismiss the angles, no matter how long or straight we draw the lines we will not have a triangle, a pastoral ministry.

I don't know of any other profession in which it is quite as easy to fake it as in ours. By adopting a reverential demeanor, cultivating a stained-glass voice, slipping occasional words like "eschatology" into conversation and *heilsgeschichte* into our discourse — not often enough actually to confuse people but enough to keep them aware that our habitual train of thought is a cut above the pew level — we are trusted, without any questions asked, as stewards of the mysteries. Most people, at least the ones that we are with most of the time, know that we are in fact surrounded by enormous mysteries: birth and death, good and evil, suffering and joy, grace, mercy, forgiveness. It takes only a hint here and a gesture there, an empathetic sigh, or a compassionate touch to convey that we are at home and expert in these deep matters. Even when in occasional fits of humility or honesty we disclaim sanctity, we are not believed. People have a need to be reassured that someone is in touch with the ultimate things. Their own interior lives are a muddle of shopping lists and good intentions, guilty adulteries (whether fantasized or actual) and episodes of heroic virtue, desires for holiness mixed with greed for self-satisfaction. They hope to do better someday beginning maybe tomorrow or at the latest next week. Meanwhile, they need someone around who can stand in for them, on whom they can project their wishes for a life pleasing to God. If we provide a bare-bones outline of pretence, they take it as the real thing and run with it, imputing to us clean hands and pure hearts.

The less personal and more public aspects of our lives are just as easy to fake. We can crib our sermons from the masters, learn to lead a liturgy by rote, write the appropriate Scriptures for home and hospital visitation in our cuffs for unobtrusive reference, memorize half a dozen prayers to suit the occasions when we are asked for a "little prayer" to get things started on the right note, and learn how to chair a committee by attending a few meetings of the PTA and making notes on what does and doesn't work.

For a long time I have been convinced that I could take a person with a high school education, give him or her a six-month trade school training, and provide a pastor who would be satisfactory to any discriminating American congregation. The curriculum would consist of four courses. *Course I:* Creative Plagiarism. I would put you in touch with a wide range of excellent and inspirational talks, show you how to alter them just enough to obscure their origins, and get you a reputation for wit and wisdom. *Course II:* Voice Control for Prayer and Counseling. We would develop your own distinct style of Holy Joe intonation, acquiring the skill in resonance and modulation that conveys an unmistakable aura of sanctity. *Course III:* Efficient Office Management. There is nothing that parishioners admire more in their pastors than the capacity to run a tight ship administratively. If we return all telephone calls within twenty-four hours, answer all letters within a week, distributing enough carbons to key people so that they know we are on top of things, and have just the right amount of clutter on our desks — not too much or we appear inefficient, not too little or we appear underemployed — we quickly get the reputation for efficiency that is far more important than anything that we actually do. *Course IV:* Image Projection. Here we would master the half-dozen well-known and easily implemented devices that create the impression that we are terrifically busy and widely sought after for counsel by influential people in the community. A one-week refresher course each year would introduce new phrases that would convince our parishioners that we are bold innovators on the cutting edge of the megatrends and at the same time solidly rooted in all the traditional values of our sainted ancestors.

(I have been laughing for several years over this trade

school training for pastors with which I plan to make my fortune. Recently, though, the joke has backfired on me. I keep seeing advertisements for institutes and workshops all over the country that invite pastors to sign up for this exact curriculum. The advertised course offerings are not quite as honestly labeled as mine, but the content appears to be identical — a curriculum that trains pastors to satisfy the current consumer tastes in religion. I'm not laughing anymore.)

⋮ ⋮ ⋮

Anne Tylor in her novel *Morgan's Passing* told the story of a middle-aged Baltimore man who passed through people's lives with astonishing aplomb and expertise in assuming roles and gratifying expectations. The novel opens with Morgan watching a puppet show on a church lawn on a Sunday afternoon. A few minutes into the show a young man comes from behind the puppet stage and asks, "Is there a doctor here?" After thirty or forty seconds of silence from the audience, Morgan stands up, slowly and deliberately approaches the young man, and asks, "What is the trouble?" The puppeteer's pregnant wife is in labor; a birth seems imminent. Morgan puts the young couple in the back of his station wagon and sets off for Johns Hopkins Hospital. Halfway there the husband cries, "The baby is coming!" Morgan, calm and self-assured, pulls to the curb, sends the about-to-be-father to the corner to buy a Sunday paper as a substitute for towels and bed sheets, and delivers the baby. He then drives to the emergency room of the hospital, puts the mother and baby safely on a stretcher, and disappears. After the excitement dies down, the couple asks for Dr. Morgan. They want to thank him. No one has ever heard of a Dr. Morgan. They are puzzled — and frustrated that they can't express their gratitude. Several months later they are pushing their baby in a stroller and see Morgan walking on the other side of the street. They run over and greet him, showing him the healthy baby that he brought into the world. They tell him how hard they had looked for him, and of the hospital's bureaucratic incompetence in tracking him down. In an unaccustomed gush of honesty he admits to them that he is not really a doctor. In fact, he runs a hardware store, but they needed a doctor and being a doctor in those circumstances was not all that difficult. It is an image thing, he tells them: you discern what people expect and fit into it. You can get by with it in all the honored professions. Morgan has been doing this all his life, impersonating doctors, lawyers, pastors, and counselors as occasions present themselves. Then he confides, "You know, I would never pretend to be a plumber, or impersonate a butcher — they would find me out in twenty seconds."[2]

Morgan was on to something that most pastors catch on to early in their work: the image aspects of being a pastor, the parts that have to do with meeting people's expectations, can be faked easily. We can impersonate a pastor without being a pastor. The problem, though, is that while we can get by with it in our communities, often with applause, we can't get by with it within ourselves. At least not all of us. Some of us get restive. We feel awful. No level of success seems to be proof against an eruption of *angst* in the middle of our applauded performance. The restiveness does not come from Puritan guilt: we *are* doing what we are paid to do. The people who pay our salaries are getting their money's worth. We are "giving good weight" — the sermons are inspiring, the committees are efficient, the morale is good. The restiveness comes from another dimension — from a vocational memory, a spiritual hunger, a professional commitment. Being the kind of pastor that satisfies

---

2. Anne Tyler, *Morgan's Passing* (New York: Alfred A. Knopf, 1980).

a congregation is one of the easiest jobs on the face of the earth — *if* we are satisfied with satisfying congregations. The hours are good, the pay is adequate, the prestige is considerable. Why don't we find it easy? Why aren't we content with it?

Because we set out to do something quite different. We set out to risk our lives in a venture of faith. We committed ourselves to a life of holiness. At some point we realized the immensity of God and of the great invisibles that socket into our arms and legs, into bread and wine, into our brains and our tools, into mountains and rivers, giving them meaning, destiny, value, joy, beauty, salvation. We responded to a call to convey these realities in word and sacrament and to give leadership to a community of faith in such a way that connected and coordinated what the men and women, children and youth in this community are doing in their work and play with what God is doing in mercy and grace. In the process we learned the difference between a profession or craft, and a job. A job is what we do to complete an assignment. Its primary requirement is that we give satisfaction to whomever makes the assignment and pays our wage. We learn what is expected and we do it. There is nothing wrong with doing jobs. To a lesser or greater extent we all have them; somebody has to wash the dishes and take out the garbage. But professions and crafts are different. In these we have an obligation beyond pleasing somebody: we are pursuing or shaping the very nature of reality, convinced that when we carry out our commitments we actually benefit people at a far deeper level than if we simply did what they asked of us.[3] In crafts we are dealing with the

---

3. ". . . professionals are autonomous men, beholden to the nature of things and the judgments of their peers, and not subject to bosses or bureaucrats but bound by an explicit or implicit oath to benefit their clients and the community." Paul Goodman, *The New Reformation* (New York: Random House, 1970), p. 47.

visible realities, in professions with invisible. The craft of wood-worker, for instance, has an obligation to the wood itself, its grain and texture. A good woodworker knows his woods and treats them with respect. Far more is involved than pleasing customers; something like integrity of material is involved. With professions the integrity has to do with the invisibles: for physicians it is health (not merely making people feel good); with lawyers, justice (not helping people get their own way); with professors, learning (not cramming cranial cavities with information on tap for examinations). And with pastors it is God (not relieving anxiety, or giving comfort, or running a religious establishment).

We all start out knowing this, or at least having a pretty good intimation of it. But when we entered our first parish we were given a job. Most of the people that we deal with most of the time are dominated by a sense of self, not a sense of God. Insofar as we also deal with their primary concern, the self — directing, counseling, instructing, encouraging — they give us good marks in our jobs as pastors. Whether we deal with God or not, they don't care overly much. Flannery O'Connor describes one pastor in such circumstances as one part minister and three parts masseuse.[4]

It is very difficult to do one thing when most of the people around us are asking us to do something quite different, especially when these people are nice, intelligent, treat us with respect, and pay our salaries. We get up each morning and the telephone rings, people meet us, letters are addressed to us — often at a tempo of bewildering urgency. All of these calls and meetings and letters are from people who are asking us to do something for them, quite apart from any belief in God. That is, they come to us not because they are looking for God but

---

4. Flannery O'Connor, *The Habit of Being,* ed. Sally Fitzgerald (New York: Farrar, Strauss, Giroux, 1979), p. 81.

because they are looking for a recommendation, or good advice, or an opportunity, and they vaguely suppose that we might be qualified to give it to them.

A number of years ago I had a knee injury that I self-diagnosed. I knew that all it needed was some whirlpool treatments. In my college years we had a whirlpool in the training room and so I had considerable experience with its effectiveness in treating my running injuries as well as making me feel good in the process. The only place in my present community where there was a whirlpool was at the physical therapist's. I called to make an appointment. He refused; I had to have a doctor's prescription. I called an orthopedic physician, went in for an examination (this was getting more complicated and expensive than I had planned), and found that he wouldn't give me the prescription for the whirlpool. He said that it wasn't the proper treatment for my injury. I protested: it certainly can't do any harm and it might do some good. His refusal was adamantine. He was a professional. His primary commitment was to some invisible abstraction called health, healing. He was not committed to satisfying my requests. His integrity, in fact, forbade him to satisfy my requests if they encroached on his primary commitment. I have since learned that by a little shopping around I could have found a doctor who would have given me the prescription that I wanted.

I reflect on that incident occasionally. Am I keeping the line clear between what I am committed to and what people are asking of me? Is my primary orientation God's grace, his mercy, his action in creation and covenant? And am I committed enough to it so that when people ask me to do something that will not lead them into a more mature participation in these realities and actions I refuse? I don't like to think of all the visits I have made, counseling given, marriages performed, meetings attended, prayers offered — one friend calls it sprinkling holy water on Cabbage Patch dolls — solely because people asked me to do it and it didn't seem at the time that it would do any harm and who knows it might do some good. Besides, I knew there was a pastor down the street who would do anything asked of him but whose theology was so wretched that he would probably do active harm in the process. My theology, at least, was evangelical and orthodox.

How do I keep the line sharp? How do I maintain a sense of pastoral vocation in the middle of a community of people who are hiring me to do religious jobs? How do I keep a sense of professional integrity in the midst of a people who are long practiced in comparative shopping and who don't get overly exercised on the fine points of pastoral integrity?

There is an old and good answer to these questions. It is not one-liner advice but immersion in a subject that used to be the core curriculum in the formation of pastors and priests. The subject went under the name of ascetical theology, what I am calling "working the angles."

Ascetical is a ruined word in this late twentieth century. C. S. Lewis's Screwtape advised his demon tempter Wormwood that one of the most effective ways of discrediting a virtue is first of all to ruin the word: introduce associations that subtly alter our feelings and perceptions so that the word no longer works the way it was intended.[5] The lexicographic demons from the Philological Arm of Our Father Below did a terrific job on *ascetic*. The word now conveys images of the emaciated, the masochistic, the misanthropic, the misogynic. Now that the

---

5. C. S. Lewis, *The Screwtape Letters* (New York: Macmillan, 1952), pp. 131ff.

word is ruined the demons don't have to bother with evidence or argument. Who of us would be pleased to have someone call us an ascetical pastor and then have the adjective grow into a reputation? Think of what it would mean: no one would invite us to share in the frivolities of a party, or join in the vicarious barbarities of a football game, or even offer to buy us a Big Mac on the way home from a late meeting. If it were known that we were ascetical — unapproachable, unworldly — we would be cut off from most of the human race, and how then would we ever manage a workable pastoral ministry?

But *ascetical* is an athlete's word. It means training for excellence. It is the practice of the disciplines that fit us for performing our very best in an event. Not many people are unmoved when seeing an athlete perform at a world-class level: winning a race, breaking a record, throwing or jumping or diving in beautifully coordinated precision. Our admiration is spontaneous when we see anyone excel in an athletic act. Every such action is backed up by years of repetitive behaviors that are the very antithesis of spontaneity. When the moment for performance comes, the well-trained athletes, ascetics every one, run or throw or jump with prowess. We applaud the results and admire (if we happen to think about it) the behind-the-scenes practices that bring them to it.

Athletic performance is in fashion in our age and so we understand and approve the whole process that brings a man or woman to the Olympic gold. Suppose, though, that in a couple of hundred years it is no longer in fashion. The training regimens that we view now with admiration would appear quite differently. G. K. Chesterton speculated that a future historian would look back and write that hundreds and thousands of young men and women all over the world "were subjected to a horrible sort of religious torture. They were forbidden . . . to indulge in wine or tobacco during certain arbitrarily fixed periods, before certain brutal fights and festivals. Bigots insisted on their rising at unearthly hours and running violently around fields."[6] Insofar as such unsympathetic views of the training disciplines of athletes were adopted by the general population the practices gradually would be neglected and the excellent performances would become less and less frequent.

Something like this has happened with ascetical theology. The training practices of our ancestors in pastoral vocations have not been carefully looked at and then discarded because they were proved inadequate; the *word* was ruined. That practically guarantees that the meaning will not be examined or understood. Smart devil.

I take it as a given that it is futile to dispute the devil on his own ground. He is too clever by half. If he has ruined the word it is probably ruined past recovery. So instead I am employing this metaphor from mathematics — "a trigonometry of ministry" — by which I hope to gain a fresh hearing for the three training practices that are basic to all pastoral work: the act of prayer, the reading of Scripture, and the practice of spiritual direction. Without these practices there can be no developing substance in pastoral work. Without an adequate "ascetic" the best of talents and best of intentions cannot prevent a thinning out into a life that becomes mostly impersonation.

If the pastors of America were asked two questions, "What do you think about God?" and "What do you want to accomplish as a pastor?" I believe that a great majority of answers would have to be judged satisfactory. But what if we are asked

---

6. G. K. Chesterton, *Twelve Types* (London: Arthur Humphreys, 1920), pp. 67-68.

a third question, "How do you go about it — what *means* do you use to bring your spiritual goals into being in your parish?" At this point the responses would range, I am quite sure, from the faddish to the trite to the silly. Pastors, by and large, have not lost touch with the best thinking about God, and they have not lost touch with the high goals of the Christian life, but they have lost touch with the trigonometry of ministry, the angles, the *means* by which the lines of the work get connected into a triangle, *pastoral* work. The pastor who has no facility in *means* buys games and gimmicks and programs without end under the illusion of being practical.

So. There is a readily available theology of ministry. We have a well-intentioned ministry. But we have an impoverished technology of ministry. Martin Thornton tells us that when he gets through reading a book on ministry he usually finds its margins littered with the initials YBH: "Yes, but how?"[7] Terrific ideas! Excellent thinking! Superb insights! Great goals! "Yes, but how?" How do I go about it? What are the actual means by which I carry out this pastoral vocation, this ordained ministry, this professional commitment to God's word and God's grace in my life and in the lives of the people to whom I preach and give the sacraments, among whom I command a life for others in the name of Jesus Christ? What connects these great realities of God and the great realities of salvation to the geography of this parish and to the chronology of this week? The answer among the masters whom I consult doesn't change: a trained attentiveness to God in prayer, in Scripture reading, in spiritual direction. This has not been tried and discarded because it didn't work, but tried and found difficult (and more than a little bit tedious) and so shelved in favor of

---

7. Martin Thornton, *The Rock and the River* (New York: Morehouse-Barlow, 1965), p. 30.

something or other that could be fit into a busy pastor's schedule.

It is common among us to hear these areas of practiced attentiveness to God in the three foundational contexts slighted on the grounds that "I have no aptitude for that sort of thing" or "My interests lie in another field." The fact is that nobody has an aptitude for it. It is hard work. It is unglamorous work. I have spent a considerable amount of time for much of my life among track and field athletes; I have never met one who liked to run laps or do push-ups. But I have met a few who were determined to win races and some who had a great desire to break records. They accepted whatever practices their coaches assigned to them so that they could do their very best with the bodies they had and so attain these excellent ends. The pastor's coaches are the spiritual/ascetical theologians. They work across a vast spectrum of cultural conditions and represent every conceivable aptitude and temperament. These people resist categorization, are impatient with labels and formulas, and continually catch us off guard with one surprise after another. They insist that there are "no dittos among souls,"[8] whether in pastors or in the people they work with. Still, underlying the flourishing of spontaneities is a pervasive consensus that none of us can mature into excellence without a lifelong persistence of trained attentiveness to God in the soul, in Israel and church, and in the neighbor as we work away at our trigonometry of prayer, Scripture, and spiritual direction.

· For the most part none of this is very exciting. It is much more fun to watch someone going to the moon than to make the machine that gets him there. It is much more challenging

---

8. Friedrich von Hugel, *Letters to a Niece,* ed. and with an introduction by Gwendolen Green (London: J. M. Dent & Sons, 1958), p. xxix.

to deliver a sermon than to develop the person who preaches it. It is far more stimulating to organize and administer a parish program crisply than to live for weeks or months in uncertainty waiting patiently for clarity of vision. "Working the angles" is what we do when nobody is watching. It is repetitive and often boring. It is blue collar, not dog collar work.

. . .
. . .
. . .

What follows is not a textbook for a "trigonometry of ministry." I am not writing formal instruction in the areas of prayer, Scripture, and spiritual direction. These have been and are being done well by many others. My intent is more modest but no less compelling: to call the attention of my brothers and sisters in pastoral ministry to what all our predecessors agreed was basic in the practice of our calling; to insist that pastoral work has no integrity unconnected with the angles of prayer, Scripture, and spiritual direction; and to offer reflections and commentary out of the context of my own work. Since no one of us takes kindly to counsel given from the safety of the sidelines when we are in the middle of difficult work, it might be important to say that all of this has been written "in the field" in a single-pastor church.

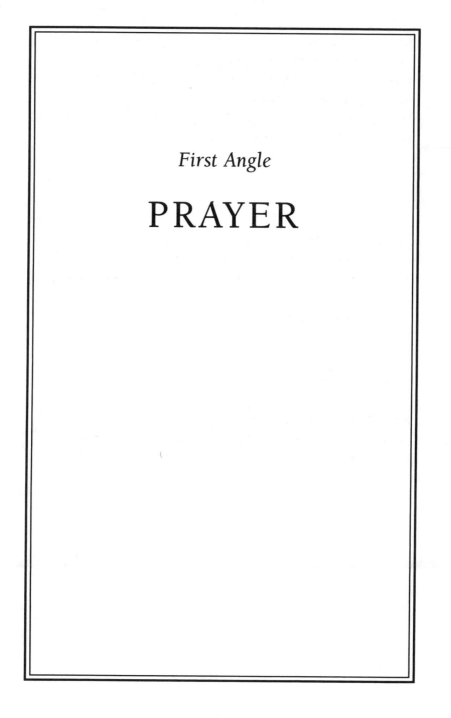

First Angle

PRAYER

I

Greek Stories and Hebrew Prayers

THE SHEER quantity of wreckage around us is appalling: wrecked bodies, wrecked marriages, wrecked careers, wrecked plans, wrecked families, wrecked alliances, wrecked friendships, wrecked prosperity. We avert our eyes. We try not to dwell on it. We whistle in the dark. We wake up in the morning hoping for health and love, justice and success, we build quick mental and emotional defenses against the inrush of bad news, and we try to keep our hopes up. And then some kind of crash or other puts us or someone we care about in a pile of wreckage. Newspapers document the ruins with photographs and headlines. Our own hearts and journals fill in the details. Are there any promises, any hopes that are exempt from the general carnage? It doesn't seem so.

Pastors walk into and through these ruins every day. Why do we do it? And what do we hope to accomplish in the ruins? After all these centuries things don't seem to have gotten much better; do we think that another day's effort is going to stay the avalanche to doomsday? Why do we all not become cynics at last? Is it sheer naiveté that keeps some pastors investing themselves in acts of compassion, inviting people to a life of sacrifice, suffering abuse in order to witness to the truth, stubbornly repeating an old hard-to-believe and much-denied story of good news in the midst of the bad news?

Is our talk of a kingdom of God within and among us and our citizenship in it anything that can be construed as the "real world"? Or are we passing on a kind of spiritual fiction analogous to the science fictions that fantasize a better world than we will ever live in? Is pastoral work mostly a matter of putting plastic flowers in people's drab lives — well-intentioned attempts to brighten a bad scene, not totally without use, but not real in any substantive or living sense?

Many people think so, and most pastors have moments when they think so. If we think so often enough we slowly but inexorably begin to adopt the majority opinion and shape our work into something manageable within the expectations of a people for whom God is not so much a person as a legend, who suppose that the kingdom will be wonderful once we get past Armageddon but we had best work right now on the terms that *this* world gives us, and who think that the Good News is nice the way greeting card verse is nice but in no way necessary to everyday life in the way that a computer manual or a job description is.

Two facts: the general environment of wreckage provides daily and powerful stimuli to us to want to repair and fix what is wrong; the secular mind makes for a steady, unrelenting pressure to readjust our conviction of what pastoral work is so that we respond to the appalling conditions around us in terms that make sense to those who are appalled.

. . .
. . .

The definition that pastors start out with, given to us in our ordination, is that pastoral work is a ministry of word and sacrament.

Word.

But in the wreckage all words sound like "mere words."
Sacrament.

But in the wreckage what difference can a little water, a piece of bread, a sip of wine make?

Yet century after century Christians continue to take certain persons in their communities, set them apart, and say, "We want you to be responsible for saying and acting among us what we believe about God and kingdom and gospel. We believe that the Holy Spirit is among us and within us. We believe that God's Spirit continues to hover over the chaos of the world's evil and our sin, shaping a new creation and new creatures. We believe that God is not a spectator in turn amused and alarmed at the wreckage of world history but a participant in it. We believe that everything, especially everything that looks like wreckage, is material that God is using to make a praising life. We *believe* all this, but we don't *see* it. We see, like Ezekiel, dismembered skeletons whitened under a pitiless Babylonian sun. We see a lot of bones that once were laughing and dancing children, of adults who once made love and plans, of believers who once brought their doubts and sang their praises in church — and sinned. We don't see the dancers or the lovers or the singers — at best we see only fleeting glimpses of them. What we see are bones. Dry bones. We see sin and judgment on the sin. That is what it *looks* like. It looked that way to Ezekiel; it looks that way to anyone with eyes to see and a brain to think; and it looks that way to us.

"But we *believe* something else. We believe in the coming together of these bones into connected, sinewed, muscled human beings who speak and sing and laugh and work and believe and bless their God. We believe that it happened the way Ezekiel preached it and we believe that it still happens. We believe it happened in Israel and that it happens in the

23

church. We believe that we are part of the happening as we sing our praises, listen believingly to God's word, receive the new life of Christ in the sacraments. We believe that the most significant thing that happens or can happen is that we are no longer dismembered but are remembered into the resurrection body of Christ.

"We need help in keeping our beliefs sharp and accurate and intact. We don't trust ourselves — our emotions seduce us into infidelities. We know that we are launched on a difficult and dangerous act of faith, and that there are strong influences intent on diluting or destroying it. We want you to help us: be our pastor, a minister of word and sacrament, in the middle of this world's life. Minister with word and sacrament to us in all the different parts and stages of our lives — in our work and play, with our children and our parents, at birth and death, in our celebrations and sorrows, on those days when morning breaks over us in a wash of sunshine, and those other days that are all drizzle. This isn't the only task in the life of faith, but it is your task. We will find someone else to do the other important and essential tasks. *This* is yours: word and sacrament.

"One more thing: we are going to ordain you to this ministry and we want your vow that you will stick to it. This is not a temporary job assignment but a way of life that we need lived out in our community. We know that you are launched on the same difficult belief venture in the same dangerous world as we are. We know that your emotions are as fickle as ours, and that your mind can play the same tricks on you as ours. That is why we are going to *ordain* you and why we are going to exact a *vow* from you. We know that there are going to be days and months, maybe even years, when we won't feel like we are believing anything and won't want to hear it from you. And we know that there will be days and

24

weeks and maybe even years when you won't feel like saying it. It doesn't matter. Do it. You are ordained to this ministry, vowed to it. There may be times when we come to you as a committee or delegation and demand that you tell us something else than what we are telling you now. Promise right now that you won't give in to what we demand of you. You are not the minister of our changing desires, or our time-conditioned understanding of our needs, or our secularized hopes for something better. With these vows of ordination we are lashing you fast to the mast of word and sacrament so that you will be unable to respond to the siren voices. There are a lot of other things to be done in this wrecked world and we are going to be doing at least some of them, but if we don't know the basic terms with which we are working, the foundational realities with which we are dealing — God, kingdom, gospel — we are going to end up living futile, fantasy lives. Your task is to keep telling the basic story, representing the presence of the Spirit, insisting on the priority of God, speaking the biblical words of command and promise and invitation."

That, or something very much like that, is what I understand the church to say to the people whom it ordains to be its pastors.

Still, no matter how impressive the ritual, no matter how sincerely the vows are given, we keep trying to untie the cords that lash us to the mast. Some of us manage to get loose and respond to other demands. When the people around us forget the terms of our ordination, forget why they asked us to be pastors in the first place, and urgently try to involve us in their newest project, we begin to lose confidence in the authority of our own hard trade. We feel left out of the mainstream and then attempt to cure our sense of exclusion, obscurity, and frustration by plunging into an action that will "make a difference."

· · ·
· · ·
· · ·

Is there anything to be done about it, some one thing that will keep us at what we set out to do and were set apart to do? If we polled our pastor colleagues, as someone every now and then does, we would get a variety of responses. One response — which would be in predictably short supply, though — would be "prayer." I don't mean that the poll would show that pastors do not pray, but rather that they don't view prayer as the central and essential act that keeps pastoral work true to itself, centered in word and sacrament. What, though, if we extended our poll to all our pastor predecessors and asked them, "What is the most important pastoral act for maintaining your identity?" G. K. Chesterton said that tradition is the only true democracy because it means giving a vote to your ancestors.[1] If we count only the votes of those who happen to be on their feet at this moment, we are letting a small minority make the decision, and a not very distinguished minority at that. Chesterton argued for extending the franchise to the cemeteries. When we do that the ballots naming "prayer" come in with an overwhelming majority. For the majority of the Christian centuries most pastors have been convinced that prayer is the central and essential act for maintaining the essential shape of the ministry to which they were ordained.

Why is this century of pastors not voting with the majority? Have conditions changed so much in our age that prayer is no longer fit to be the formative act? Have developments in theology shown other things to be central and prayer at the periphery? Or have we let ourselves be distracted, diverted,

---

1. G. K. Chesterton, *Orthodoxy* (New York: John Lane, 1908), p. 85.

and seduced? I think we have. And I think there is a story that shows how it happened.

$$\begin{matrix} \bullet & \bullet & \bullet \\ \bullet & \bullet & \bullet \\ \bullet & \bullet & \bullet \end{matrix}$$

When we attempt to orient ourselves in reality, we can rarely do better than go to the Greeks for help. The Greeks lived passionately and intelligently. They tried to understand what it means to live in a world in which things are always going wrong. With their marvelous imaginations they put their understanding into stories. The Greeks were the best storytellers the world has ever known. We keep telling their stories to each other to locate ourselves in the human condition. The stories of Odysseus and Achilles, of Oedipus and Electra, of Narcissus and Sisyphus are diagnostic as we try to get our bearings and keep our balance. The story that helps us understand the loss of prayer in pastoral work is the story of Prometheus.

Aeschylus tells this story best.[2] According to him the essential characteristic of the human being in the early days of the race was that each person knew the day of his or her death. That is to say, we knew our limits. Mortality was not a vague apprehension but a fixed date on the calendar. In such a condition and with such knowledge there was no incentive to do much more than exist. On top of that, the gods were capricious and brutal. They had the knowledge of how things worked and the means to accomplish them, but they shared neither their knowledge nor their means. They were neither generous nor fair. They held all the significant cards in their own hands. So what is the use of trying? The basic human experience is of mortality and tyranny.

---

2. *The Complete Greek Tragedies,* ed. David Grene and Richmond Lattimore (Chicago: University of Chicago Press, 1959), 1:311-51.

Prometheus, one of the gods, somehow became compassionately concerned about our plight and correspondingly angry at Zeus, the chief of the gods. He took it upon himself to do something about changing the human condition for the better. He did three things that would make a difference. First, he "caused mortals to cease foreseeing doom." That is, he took away the knowledge of the day of death, the sense of limits, the awareness of mortality. Freed from a debilitating sense of doom, the human now could attempt anything. Second, he "placed in them blind hopes." Prometheus instilled incentive in men and women to be more than they were, to reach out, to stretch themselves, to be ambitious. But the incentives were blind and directionless, unrelated to any reality. And third, Prometheus stole fire from the gods and gave it to humanity. With this gift, people were able to cook food, make weapons, fire pottery. The entire world of technology opened up.

By this act, Prometheus set us on the way we have continued: unmindful of limits, setting goals unrelated to the actual conditions of our humanity, and possessing the technical means to change the conditions under which we live. We don't have to put up with things as they are. Things can be better; we have the means to accomplish whatever we want to do. Fire provided the energy that became technology — the machine. Consequently, we humans don't know that we are human; rather, we think we are gods and act like gods. The awareness of our mortality is lost to us. A sensitivity to the results of our actions is lost to us. That would not be so bad if we did not have fire, the technical means to act out our illusions of divinity. As it is we have the technology of the gods without the wisdom of the gods, without the foresight of the gods.

Zeus, of course, was furious. He punished Prometheus by chaining him to a rock in a remote mountain, exposed to the scorching sun and the cold moon. Every day vultures attacked him, tearing at his innards, eating his liver. Each night the liver would grow back, ready for the next day's rapacious assault. Prometheus is unrepentant. He has brought fire to humankind. He is defiant. He suffers. The story is tragic. The bringing of fire, enlightenment, and technology to humankind makes it possible for us to live civilized lives; at the same time it is the source of suffering. The very act that makes it possible for us to rise above our brutish lives is the cause of unimaginable suffering of a new order.

Prometheus: daring, bold, compassionate, intelligent — raising the standard of living, expanding the scope of living, deepening the resources for living. But bound: chained to the rock showing the consequences of trying to improve the human condition by giving us ambition and tools without at the same time giving us foresight and training us in self-knowledge. It is the story of Western civilization: incredible progress in things, defiantly unmindful of the nature of our humanity, unimaginable suffering in persons. A powerful story. A true story. Werner Jaeger calls the Prometheus myth the greatest expression of the tragedy of our own nature.[3]

The Prometheus story exhibits the human condition as a tragedy: *this* is the way life is. It does not suggest a solution. The power of the story is the realization that there is no solution. This is fate. Progress in technology is inevitably connected with an increase in anxious suffering. But we have no stomach for tragedy. We want *solutions*. The recurring fantasy is that with the aid of the computer we will make a quantum leap technologically and solve the problems of the age. Just a little more fire from the gods and we will get the world running right after all. Counter voices raise the antitechnology solution: reduce technology, learn

---

3. Werner Jaeger, *Paideia: The Ideals of Greek Culture*, trans. Gilbert Highet (New York: Oxford University Press, 1945), 1:263.

to live within limits, relearn the meaning of the day of our death, respect persons more than things — the humanist way.

Our age is very Promethean. No more so than earlier ages, perhaps, but with this difference: the tragic story of Prometheus is not well known among us. Earlier generations posted it as a warning. They told the Prometheus *story* as an antidote to the Promethean *spirit*. The reality of the tragedy was kept alive in the consciousness of the people by poets and novelists, philosophers and artists. But modern philosophers have abandoned what Plato set as the agenda of philosophy, namely, the study of death. The mass of people have their sense of reality shaped by commercials and publicists who promise pain-free longevity. Our society dismisses the artists and writers who deepen our awareness of the tragic dimensions of existence. Modern mythmakers have revised and condensed the story of Prometheus and tell it not as a tragedy but as a triumph. The bowdlerized version takes the single element of stealing fire from the gods, that is, the inauguration of technology, energy, and tools, and celebrates this as a gateway to utopia. The other parts of the story — amnesia regarding death, unguided ambition, the daily renewed suffering that is a consequence of living without wisdom in defiance of our human nature — are edited out.

Our pastoral ancestors self-consciously set themselves in opposition to this Promethean spirit and understood their work as proceeding from a very different source, from prayer: cultivating a grace-filled relationship with God, not defiantly plotting an ambitious rivalry against him. Because of this different source action, death was viewed differently. There were times, in fact, when pastoral work was defined as preparing people for a good death.[4] When the Promethean spirit blurred or

------

4. See, e.g., Sister Mary Catherine O'Connor, *The Art of Dying Well: The Development of the "Ars Moriendi"* (New York: Columbia University Press, 1942).

eliminated an awareness of mortality, the pastor's task was to bring it back into focus. The meditated consideration of death is important because it teaches wisdom: how to live as a *human*, not as a *god;* how to live into and up to human limits but not beyond them. "So teach us to number our days that we may get a heart of wisdom," cried the psalmist (Ps. 90:12). Luther called out in response, "Lord! that we all might be such skilled arithmeticians!"[5]

But the old phrase "preparing for a good death" has been expurgated from pastoral work. We have let ourselves be co-opted in the struggle against limits, committed to raising the standard of living: bigger machines, cheaper chicken. We ourselves have become Promethean — working in a good cause, compassionately helping people, but uncritically using the means offered by the world. Our motives are of the best. But the effort is defiant, assertive, cheerlessly compulsive — a struggle against fate on behalf of poor, dying, bereft, and benighted humans. And why should we not do it with the means so uncritically applauded and so readily at hand? Technology makes things happen and promises to eliminate poverty, pain, boredom. When someone raises the point that there is more poverty, pain, and boredom today than our planet has ever known, the speech is interrupted within five minutes by the breathless announcement of some incredible technological breakthrough, and we are so dazzled by the achievement that we are distracted from noticing the consequences. With the best wills in the world but the poorest memories we have joined in the struggle to make life better for everyone with any available means. There is so much to do, there are so many limits to be broken through, and there is, right on our doorsteps, a

---

5. Martin Luther, *Luther's Works,* ed. Jaroslav Pelikan (St. Louis: Concordia, 1956), 13:128.

Promethean technology to help us do it. Prometheus, of course, does not pray; there is too much to *do* and there is too little time to do it.

• • •
• • •

At the same time that the Promethean spirit has been subverting pastoral work by devaluating prayer's formative action, another element has been quietly in alliance with it. This element is no less insidious for being less conspicuous. The swashbuckling story of a Greek god accounts for the first element of subversion; the bookish work of a German scholar accounts for the second, which involved a rewriting of Hebrew history in such a way that prayer was pushed out of the action.

The last century experienced a radical reassessment of biblical history. This new historical approach had its origin among the Enlightenment *philosophes* of the seventeenth and eighteenth centuries. In that company of learned men — led by Kant in Germany, Voltaire in France, Gibbon in England — there was a great surge of curiosity and enthusiasm for everything earthly and human, accompanied by a marked aversion to anything divine and heavenly. "Enough of medieval speculation on angels and eternity," they said. "The urgent agenda is the minds and bodies of people, how we think and behave, what we have actually done in history." In the field of history everything was looked at with critical and skeptical eyes and rewritten with a rigor that attempted to exclude superstition, legend, myth, and propagandizing lies. Previous to the Enlightenment, history had been written with some kind of scheme in mind. History was not for its own sake, simply writing down what happened, but was in the service of God, or Nation, or Morality. History was written to show God working out his purposes, or Fate working out some impersonal principle, or

Morality working itself out in the affairs of the human race, or how this king was superior to all others. History writing ranged between the poles of propaganda and gullibility. Around the propaganda pole history was written tendentiously — evidence was sorted through and selected to support whatever moral or religious or political cause was in favor. Around the gullibility pole anything that was reported or gossiped — ghosts, unicorns, portents — was solemnly written down. Real history was also written, of course, but it was adulterated with the propaganda and the gossip — sometimes more, sometimes less, and with no one seeming to care very much about the more or less.

In the Enlightenment decades this changed. Historians took a hard look at the well-known fact that people lie a lot, and that they don't quit lying when they take up literary or scholarly or religious pursuits. People make up stories to make themselves look better and they make up stories to make their God or gods look better. The new historians asked the question: "How would these old histories read if we took into account these tendencies to propagandize for a cause and gossip about the miraculous, and subject everything to a critical methodology that culls out the lies and half-lies?" That became the program.

One of the famous applications of the new method was Edward Gibbon's rewriting of the history of the late Roman empire and early Christianity. The accepted view had been that the Roman empire fell through a process of moral disintegration, while the church rose to ascendancy on the strength of its moral fervor and holy life. Gibbon's version turned that upside down. He wrote the story to show that the noble Roman life was enervated by Christian parasitism. It wasn't sin that put the great Roman empire into decline but religious silliness. When people started taking a god more seriously than their godlike selves, the grand human achievement that Rome had brought to near perfection fell into disrepair through sheer neglect. It was as if the owners of a great country house who had for generations improved their buildings and cultivated their grounds with lavish care suddenly started going to the race track and betting money on the horses, losing interest in their house and land, letting them fall into shameful disrepair. Except for the Romans it wasn't the race track and a horse that drew them into irresponsibility; it was the church and the Christ.

Chapter after chapter of ancient history was subjected to these critical methods. There was a jackpot of benefits: knowledge of what it means to be human was extended back into time through a variety of cultures and civilizations. But the results were not always as truthful or as factual as they at first seemed. Sometimes the new historian merely substituted a new ideological bias for the old one, but escaped immediate detection under the cover of scientific objectivity. "Scholarly objectivity" in the Enlightenment era intimidated readers into uncritical acceptance quite as much as "divine inspiration" had earlier.

By the nineteenth century these methods were brought to bear on the historical parts of Scripture. The belief that the Scriptures were divinely inspired and therefore authoritative had exempted them from historical-critical examination for a century or so, but the time came when they were no longer exempt. It was not to be tolerated, said the new scholars, that Scripture hide behind the skirts of doctrine. She was subpoenaed and made to face the same court of inquiry as the secular documents. Truth was the goal; if the Christian faith were true it had nothing to fear and everything to gain by employing methods that had no other aim than to discover and describe what actually happened in contrast to happenings that people wrongfully remembered or wishfully hoped or tendentiously rearranged.

The most famous name in this reconstruction of biblical history is Julias Wellhausen. As a result of his reconstruction, the Psalms, the Hebrew prayers, lost their central importance and ended up on the edge of the historical scene. Up to this time the Psalms had been at the very center of the action, as they showed the Hebrews in bold and vigorous prayer, responding to the God who was shaping salvation in them. They were taken with great seriousness and great delight. They attracted the best commentators. They provided a language for expressing the entire life of worship and every dimension of experience in the people of faith. The human dimensions of the biblical story were nowhere seen in so much detail and depth as here. The praying person was the person responding out of the detailed concreteness of the human condition to the totality of the divine presence. Then, with a stroke of his pen, Wellhausen took the Psalms out of the action, displacing them from the dynamic and creative parts of history. His work was so thoroughgoing and the ripple effect was so far-reaching that the name Wellhausen takes its place alongside Prometheus in accounting for the displacement of prayer from its formerly assured center.

The Wellhausian reconstruction described Hebrew history in three stages. In the first stage its beginnings are shrouded in the midst of prehistory: legendary Abraham clumsily groped his way through shadows of superstition and child sacrifice. Crude tribal cults in Palestine, murderous and fanatic, gradually evolved toward a semblance of civilization, picking up bits and pieces of morality from their advanced Egyptian and Babylonian neighbors. Stories developed around odd physical features in the landscape and natural disasters and were given a moral or spiritual tilt. Interpretations of divine or demonic powers were worked into the storytelling. Across the centuries, out of this melting pot of nomadic drifters, something like a nation gradually emerged, a nation with a penchant for talking about God.

Then out of this unpromising milieu something truly spectacular happened: the prophets emerged into the light of history. *Emerged* is too mild a word — *exploded* was more like it. This was the second stage. Isaiah and Amos, Hosea and Jeremiah were giants in the land, passionate in their monotheism, urgent in their morality, with a burning vision of justice. The world had never seen anything quite like it. These prophets strode through the cities and across the countryside confronting and denouncing, rousing the human spirit to unprecedented moral heights and giving new shape to the political, economic, and social orders. This was religion at its best, religion evolved out of the lower orders of superstition, cult legend, and myth into mature, monotheistic morality.

The third stage came after a series of military disasters and a terrible exile left the Hebrews oppressed and demoralized. They lost all political identity. The prophetic movement lost momentum and ran down. The incredible vigor dissipated. With the disappearance of the great prophets a spiritual lassitude overcame the people. They declined into a people who told stories of the good old days through a filter of nostalgia. Out of old legends and slivers of historical memory they fashioned heroic figures on the prophetic model: Abraham courageous in faith, Moses wise and fearless, David lyrical and tough. What else was there to do but tell stories? Well, they could also pray. So they prayed. They had been moved off of the stage of history; there was nothing else to do but pray. Tell stories and pray. The Psalms, then, are their prayers. They are the pious residue of a once vigorous faith. The powerful, passionate, life-changing, society-reforming energy of the prophets was now gone; in their place were the pathetic prayers of a once proud people, old men and little children cultivating an inward piety to compensate for their lost and remembered glory.

That, in rough outline, is the revised history. Stage one, beginnings in a prehistory of crude superstition and crudely warring tribes, formulated later in sagas and myths. Stage two, a brilliant flowering of moral passion in the great prophets. Stage three, a weak dénouement into a defeated, whining piety, expressed in the Psalms.

At the end of the century, in 1899, Bernard Duhm published his influential commentary on the Psalms.[6] He dated all of them during the Maccabean Period (167–63 B.C.), with the single exception of the exilic Psalm 137. Duhm's position was supported by the greatest Psalms scholar of the day, Hermann Gunkel, and was from that time accepted as both obvious and irrefutable.

None of these scholars intended anything invidious in their work — most of them were devout men who loved the Psalms. They were, most of them, simply following the paths of Enlightenment scholarship, uncritically convinced that this was the path to truth. They did not intend to sabotage the life of prayer. But the unintended consequence was that the Psalms were effectively removed from the action. Instead of being seen as the centerpiece in the cultivation of faith, the action-shaping school of prayer in which men and women learned to give answer out of every part of their being to the God who was calling all creation and all redemption into existence, the Psalms were regarded as the decrepit pieties of a religion that had spent itself.

With the Psalms so regarded historically, prayer in general did not long escape a similar verdict. If this is the place of prayer in the historical development of our faith, it will not attract a large following among people who want to do some-

---

6. Bernard Duhm, *Die Psalmen* (KHAR XIV Frieburg, 1899), p. 72.

thing about what is wrong with the world. The person we prefer to watch and emulate is the prophet. The most vigorous expression of a biblical ministry is in prophetic preaching and political confrontation, calling people to account in the streets, challenging corrupt authority, speaking God's counsel with eloquent passion. The Psalms are nice as texts to anthems and as mottos for wall hangings. Prayer is useful at the end of the day to calm the frazzled spirit and compose ourselves for a night of rest. If prophecy is the steak and potatoes of religion, prayer is a warm glass of milk to encourage tranquil sleep.

Whether pastors ever consciously adopt this Wellhausian reconstruction of biblical history and its consequent denigration of the Psalms as dynamically central to the life of faith is moot: the Psalms and prayer are, in fact, marginal in pastoral education and practice. Julias Wellhausen played a significant part in this marginalization. In twentieth-century America the prophetic pastor of action and the managerial pastor are the ministry role models; the prayerful pastor leading people in worship draws, at best, a yawn. But Wellhausen, it turns out, was not the last word. He was a brilliant scholar and much of what he did continues to be developed and built upon by other scholars. Yet one part of his work, the historical reconstruction, fell apart completely. It did so rather quietly, and a lot of pastors, it seems, have not heard the news of the debacle. One completely unexpected but most interesting detail of this has particular cogency for pastors and for the church at prayer. It was set in motion when the Norwegian scholar Sigmund Mowinckel entered the field that had been pioneered by Wellhausen and Gunkel. At the same time that Mowinckel was engaged in his biblical studies, he was also working in a parallel but nonbiblical field, studying the worship of early Teutonic tribes. The two studies — the Hebrews at prayer and the Teutons at prayer — alongside one another proved catalytic and resulted in a complete overthrow of the Wellhausian verdict. The negative conclusions on the Psalms — that their historical setting was late, that their spiritual meaning was minor — were demonstrated to be dead wrong. Mowinckel's work restored the Psalms to the center of the action.[7]

In studying the Teutonic prayers Mowinckel realized that in the primitive societies of Europe the role of the community at prayer was formative in everything else that took place. When the people gathered to join their prayers in the act of worship this act was neither haphazard nor peripheral; it was dramatic and basic. "It embraced the whole of society in its powerful grip, molding ideas, instructing values and acting as a cement to bind the community together."[8] The prayers of the people were the most important things that they did. The prayers were deeply personal in their impact and shaped the life of the community in its history and culture. The pioneer in noticing this and realizing its significance was the Danish anthropologist Vilhelm Gronbech.[9] Mowinckel applied these insights to early Hebrew history and demonstrated that they were just as true there.

This led to a complete reversal in the judgment of scholars as to the place of the Psalms in the life of Israel. Wellhausen's work viewed prophecy as the creative wellspring in Israel that as it dried up left a few puddles of Psalms around. The work of Mowinckel showed the opposite: the Psalms were the artesian original, the prayer and worship out of which prophecy developed. The Psalms that had been admired for their literary qualities — damned, actually, with faint praise — and relegated

---

7. Ronald E. Clements, *One Hundred Years of Old Testament Interpretation* (Philadelphia: Westminster Press, 1976), pp. 76-98.

8. Ibid., p. 83.

9. Vilhelm Gronbech, *The Culture of the Teutons* (Oxford, 1931).

to a strictly subordinate and secondary position in the history of religion now were recognized to be basic — the *source* of what impresses us most in Israel. Ronald Clements summarizes the turnaround: for decades the Psalms

> were looked upon simply as reflecting the undercurrent of personal piety and hope which flourished when the main creative impulses of Israel's religion had ebbed away. As a result of the work of Gunkel and Mowinckel, however, the Psalms were elevated to a new position of priority as a witness to the groundwork of cult and piety which underlie the formation of the historical books as well as the phenomenon of prophecy in Israel . . . a remarkably central position.[10]

In short, the Psalms provide the language, the aspirations, the energy for the community as it comes together in prayer, and they then call into being and are formative for the activities of prophets, wise men, and historians. The Psalms initiate; the prophets follow. The inner action of prayer takes precedence over the outer action of proclamation.

The implication of this for pastoral work is plain: it begins in prayer. Anything creative, anything powerful, anything *biblical,* insofar as we are participants in it, originates in prayer. Pastors who imitate the preaching and moral action of the prophets without also imitating the prophets' deep praying and worship so evident in the Psalms are an embarrassment to the faith and an encumbrance to the church.

∴ ∴

The Promethean story and the Wellhausian historiography account for the eclipse of prayer among those who want to make a

---

10. Clements, *One Hundred Years,* p. 95.

difference in a ruined world. But we need more than an accounting; we need a strategy for doing something about it. For this we go not to our cultural ancestors, the Greeks, but to our faith ancestors, the Hebrews. The Hebrews were not so much interested in understanding the human condition as they were in responding to the divine reality. Their supreme effort was to hear God's word, not to tell stories about gods. Their characteristic speech form was not the myth but the prayer. They were deeply committed to a way of life that pivoted on the acts of God.

There *was* something to be done about the human condition, but it was not primarily what men and women attempted but what God is doing. In order to get in on that action they prayed. Their purpose was not to understand what was going on in the human race but to be a part of what was going on with God. The Greeks were experts on understanding existence from a human point of view; the Hebrews were experts in setting human existence in response to God. Whereas the Greeks had a story for every occasion, the Hebrews had a prayer for every occasion. For pastors, the Greek stories are useful, but the Hebrew prayers are essential. Prayer means that we deal first with God and then with the world. Or, that we experience the world first not as a problem to be solved but as a reality in which God is acting.

The Greek stories are the best stories in the world, interesting and accurate. They account for our condition — but they do not change it, or even promise that it can be changed. But as that great Hebrew heretic prophet of the last century, Karl Marx, put it, the point is not to understand history but to change it. If we are out to recover our original integrity, it is going to be through a recovery of prayer. If we skip the prayer, or allow ourselves to be stampeded into activities other than prayer, we end up in the tragic impasse that the Prometheus myth describes so exactly.

II

Praying by the Book

PRAYER IS A daring venture into speech that juxtaposes our words with the sharply alive words that pierce and divide souls and spirit, joints and marrow, pitilessly exposing every thought and intention of the heart (Heb. 4:12-13; Rev. 1:16). If we had kept our mouths shut we would not have involved ourselves in such a relentlessly fearsome exposure. If we had been content to speak to the women and men and children in the neighborhood we could have gotten by with using words in ways that would have them thinking well of us while concealing what we preferred to keep to ourselves. But when we venture into prayer, every word may, at any moment, come to mean just what it *means* and involve us with a holy God who wills our holiness. All we had counted on was some religious small talk, a little numinous gossip, and we are suddenly involved, without intending it and without having calculated the consequences, in something *eternal*.

That is why so many of the old masters counsel caution: Be slow to pray. This is not an enterprise to be entered into lightly. When we pray we are using words that bring us into proximity with words that break cedars, shake the wilderness, make the oaks whirl, and strip forests bare (Ps. 29:5-9). When we pray we use words that may well leave us quavering, soul-shattered, on our faces: "Woe is me! For I am lost; for I am a man of unclean lips . . . !" (Isa. 6:5). When we pray we have a more than average chance of ending up in a place that we quite definitely never wanted to be, angrily protesting, preferring death to the kind of life that God insists on recklessly throwing us into: "O Lord, take my life from me, I beseech thee, for it is better for me to die than to live" (Jon. 4:3). We want life on our conditions, not on God's conditions. Praying puts us at risk of getting involved in God's conditions. Be slow to pray. Praying most often doesn't get us what we want but what God wants, something quite at variance with what we conceive to be in our best interests. And when we realize what is going on, it is often too late to go back. Be slow to pray.

Knowing all this — that prayer is dangerous, that it moves our language into potencies we are unaccustomed to and unprepared for — it continually puzzles me that so much prayer sounds so limp, that prayer is often so utterly banal. The limpness and banality may be no more common in pastors than in laypeople, but they are more conspicuous in pastors, who are more often on public display.

Question: How does it happen that language used at the height of its powers comes out of pastoral mouths stagnant and stale?

Answer: It has been uprooted from the soil of the word of God. These so-called prayers are cut-flower words, arranged in little vases for table decorations. As long as they are artificially provided for with a container of water, they give a touch of beauty. But not for long: soon they drop and are discarded. Such flowers are often used as the centerpiece for a dinner table. They are lovely in these settings. But they are never mistaken for the real business of the table, the beef and potatoes that promise full bellies and calories for a hard day's work.

Pastors routinely, by virtue of our work and what other people think of as our work, are called upon to pray in ceremonial and decorative ways. We open meetings with prayer. We lead congregations in prayer. Sometimes we begin the day with prayer. When we are invited to community affairs — school graduations, patriotic celebrations, building dedications — our usual assignment, to give the invocation, is given top billing in the printed programs. Prayer gets things started off on the right foot. In the course of our daily work we are repeatedly involved in offering prayers in these "beginning" contexts: a child is born and we pray a thanksgiving for this beginning life; in the hospital we pray in petition as the physician begins his surgery; a person begins the slide into death, the end that is also a beginning, and we are called in to pray. It very much looks as if these prayers, placed as they are as the first item on the agendas, offered at the outset of the programs, associated with all sorts and conditions of beginnings both personal and public, are the basic act, the first word in the matter.

But appearances mislead, and insofar as we are misled our prayers lack soil for rootage and nutrient. Pastors as a class contribute a disproportionate number to the company of the misled. Why don't they know better? Why are they so easily duped? Is it vanity or ignorance that sets them up in these postures of banal pomposity? The cure, in either case, is a transplant from the weedy gravel pits of religious chatter into the soil of the word of God.

The appearances mislead: prayer is never the first word; it is always the second word. God has the first word. Prayer is answering speech; it is not primarily "address" but "response." Essential to the practice of prayer is to fully realize this secondary quality. It is especially important in the pastoral practice of prayer since pastors are so frequently placed in positions in which it appears that our prayers have an initiating energy in them, the holy words that legitimize and bless the secular prose of committee work or community discussion or getting well or growing up.

One of the indignities to which pastors are routinely subjected is to be approached, as a group of people are gathering for a meeting or a meal, with the request, "Reverend, get things started for us with a little prayer, will ya?" It would be wonderful if we would counter by bellowing William McNamara's fantasized response: "I will not! There are no *little* prayers! Prayer enters the lion's den, brings us before the holy where it is uncertain whether we will come back alive or sane, for 'it is a fearful thing to fall into the hands of a living God.'"[1]

I am not prescribing rudeness: the bellow does not have to be audible. I am insisting that the pastor who in indolence or ignorance is politely compliant with requests from congregation or community for cut-flower prayers forfeits his or her calling. Most of the people we meet, inside and outside the church, think prayers are harmless but necessary starting pistols that shoot blanks and get things going. They suppose that the "real action," as they call it, is in the "things going" — projects and conversations, plans and performances. It is an outrage and a blasphemy when pastors adjust their practice of prayer to accommodate these inanities.

The irony in all this is that by putting prayer in the apparent first place we contribute to its actual diminishment. By uttering a prayer to "get things started" we legitimize and bless a thin and callow secularism — everyone is now free to

---

1. William McNamara, O.C.D., *The Human Adventure* (Garden City, NY: Doubleday & Co., Image Books, 1976), p. 89.

go his or her own way without thinking about God any more. *"That,* at least, is out of the way; now we can get to the important things that require our attention. We have pleased God with our piety and are free to get on with the things that concern *us."*

Pastors are not responsible for bringing about this state of affairs, but when we perpetuate it by our compliance we become culpable. The moment we realize the extent of our responsibility we must do something about it. What do we do?

We do the obvious: we restore prayer to its context in God's word. Prayer is not something we think up to get God's attention or enlist his favor. Prayer is *answering* speech. The first word is God's word. Prayer is a human word and is never the first word, never the primary word, never the initiating and shaping word simply because *we* are never first, never primary. We do not honor prayer by treating it as something that it is not, even when that something is, as we suppose, sacred and exalted. What we do, in fact, is make prayer into a verbal idol. It then becomes a tool that works our diminishment and maybe even our damnation. Since, by virtue of our pastoral work, we so often find ourselves in situations in which everyone around is quite sure that prayer is, or at least should be, the first word, we must develop within ourselves the means for a full and continuous awareness of its secondary quality, its *answering* character. Otherwise we drift unaware into verbal idolatry and its consequent diminishments. We require repeated and forceful reminders: the first word is everywhere and always God's word to us, not ours to him. Vigilant attentiveness is necessary to keep our weapons sharp against these barbarian prayers that are requested and preferred by nearly everyone we meet.

We hone our attentiveness on the strop of Genesis. In creation God has the first word. Genesis describes the work of creation "in the beginning" by means of speech: "God said, 'Let

47

there be light'; and there was light." The word is repeated: God said . . . God said . . . God said . . . God said. . . . The repetitions are architectonic. Nine times through the six days of creation the phrase is uttered, *vayomer elohim,* "and God said." The word that God speaks originates, initiates, shapes, provides, orders, commands, and blesses.

God's word is the creative means by which everything comes into existence. The word of God constitutes the total reality in which we find ourselves. Everything we see and feel and deal with — sea and sky, codfish and warblers, sycamores and carrots — originates by means of this word. Everything, absolutely everything, was *spoken* into being. "For he spoke, and it came to be; he commanded, and it stood forth" (Ps. 33:9).

This is no less true of God's parallel work, redemption. St. John, in his masterful rewriting of Genesis, wrote, "In the beginning was the Word . . . and the Word became flesh." The gospel spells out in detail Jesus *speaking* salvation into being: rebuking the chaos of demons, separating men and women from damnation by calling them by name into lives of discipleship, defeating the tempter with citations of Scripture, commanding healings, using words of blessing to feed and help. The *word* is as foundational in the work of salvation as it is in the work of creation. Just as everything outside us originates in the word of God, so does everything inside us. We can't get behind the word of God. There is no human insight, no human desire, no human cry anterior to this word of God. There is no great abstraction, no great truth behind or previous to this word. Everywhere we look, everywhere we probe, everywhere we listen we come upon *word* — and it is God's word, not ours.

This massive, overwhelming *previousness* of God's speech to our prayers, however obvious it is in Scripture, is not immediately obvious to us simply because we are so much more aware of ourselves than we are of God. We are far more self-conscious than God-conscious and so when we pray, what we are ordinarily conscious of is that we are getting in the first word with God. But our consciousness lies.

So it requires effort — repeated, imaginative, biblically shaped effort — to acquire and maintain our awareness of this unqualified, thoroughgoing previousness of God's speech to anything and everything that comes out of our mouths.

Our personal experience in acquiring language is congruent with the biblical witness and provides an accessible and inexpensive laboratory for verifying Genesis and John. Because we learned language so early in our lives we have no clear memory of the process, but by observing our own children learning to speak we readily enough confirm the obvious: language is spoken into us; we learn language by being spoken to. We are plunged at birth into a sea of language. We swim in words. We are soaked in nouns and verbs. Gradually we realize that some of these words are directed to us — personally targeted words that name, love, and comfort. Then slowly, syllable by syllable, we acquire the capacity to answer: mama, papa, bottle, blanket, yes, no. Not one of these words was a first word. Hundreds of thousands of words, for days and weeks and months, were spoken to us before we began to answer, to speak our own words. All speech is answering speech. We were all spoken to before we spoke.

This language that we learn is immensely complex. It is a continuous marvel that we become adept so early at selecting, combining, and varying all the elements of sound and silence, gesture and scream, laughter and tears into appropriate responses to more and more people who are saying more and more things to us. At some point we find ourselves answering God; the usual way to describe this use of language is with the word *prayer.* Prayer is language used to respond to the most that has been said to us, with the potential for saying all that is in us. Prayer is the development of speech into maturity, language in process of being adequate to answer the one who has spoken most comprehensively to us, namely, God. Put this way, it is clear that prayer is not a narrow use of language for special occasions but the broadest use of language into which everything that is truly human in us — all the parts of our creation and salvation — comes to mature expression. But we live in a culture that has little interest in this language. We live in a society in which language is constantly being eroded and reduced.

Question: Where can we go to learn our language as it develops into maturity, as it answers God?

Answer: The Psalms.

The great and sprawling university that Hebrews and Christians have attended to learn to answer God, to learn to pray, has been the Psalms. More people have learned to pray by matriculating in the Psalms than any other way. The Psalms were the prayer book of Israel; they were the prayer book of Jesus; they are the prayer book of the church. At no time in the Hebrew and Christian centuries (with the possible exception of our own twentieth century) have the Psalms not been at the very center of all concern and practice in prayer.

There is one large fact about the Psalms that requires notice before attending to the actual reading and praying of them — their arrangement. One hundred and fifty psalms are arranged in five books. The arrangement is impossible to miss, but, like many other obvious but familiar things, we commonly fail to notice it. But *notice* is what is required: the five-book arrangement establishes the conditions under which we will pray, shaping a canonical context for prayer. If we are ignorant of or forget these conditions and context we will get almost nothing right. Mindful of the conditions and context we will never be too far wrong. The significance of the five-book arrangement cannot be over-stressed. It is not a minor and incidental matter of editorial tinkering; it is a major matter of orientation so that prayer will be learned properly as human *answering* speech to the *addressing* speech of God, and not be confused or misunderstood as initiating speech.

The separation into five books is accomplished by a stock liturgical formula with variations. The first occurrence of the formula is after Psalm 41:

> Blessed be the Lord, the God of Israel,
> > from everlasting to everlasting!
> > Amen and Amen.
> > > (41:13)

The second occurrence gathers Psalms 42 through 72 into a second book. The first sentence of blessing is identical and the concluding double Amen is identical, but the center is expanded. An additional footnote notation states that this concludes the Davidic section of the Psalter.

> Blessed be the Lord, the God of Israel,
> > who alone does wondrous things.
> Blessed be his glorious name for ever;
> > may his glory fill the whole earth!
> Amen and Amen!
>
> The prayers of David, the son of Jesse, are ended.
> > (72:18-20)

Psalms 73 through 89 are bound into the third book by the liturgical formula abbreviated to its bare essentials:

> Blessed be the Lord for ever!
> Amen and Amen.
> > (89:52)

The formula that binds Psalms 90 to 106 into a fourth book begins identically but is then intensified. The formulaic double Amen is expanded into "And let all the people say, 'Amen!'" And the accustomed final Amen is replaced by "Praise the Lord!" (the Hebrew *Hallelujah*).

> Blessed be the Lord, the God of Israel,
>> from everlasting to everlasting!
> And let all the people say, "Amen!"
>> Praise the Lord!
>>> (106:48)

The ending of the fifth book is a double conclusion. It binds Psalms 107 through 150 into a book, but it does more, by ending the Psalter itself. In order to accomplish this, the usual formula ("Blessed . . . Amen") is abandoned and a new one fashioned out of the Hallelujah as more suitable for this larger work. The word *Hallelujah* was introduced in the fourth conclusion as a supplement to the stock Amen. This Hallelujah now takes over. The shift from Amen to Hallelujah modulates the great Amen-affirmations of the first four books into a celebrative conclusion to the five-book Psalter. This grand conclusion bursts the confines of the liturgical formula and booms out five hallelujah psalms (146-50), one for each "book" of the Psalter. Each of these five concluding psalms begins and ends with the Hallelujah. Between the bracketing Hallelujahs fresh contents for praise are introduced and various dimensions of praise are developed. The last psalm, the 150th, not only begins and ends but pivots each sentence on the Hallelujah: praise the Lord, praise God, praise him . . . thirteen times — a cannonade of hallelujahs, booming salvos of joy.

> Praise the Lord!
> Praise God in his sanctuary;

praise him in his mighty firmament!
Praise him for his mighty deeds;
    praise him according to his exceeding greatness!

Praise him with trumpet sound;
    praise him with lute and harp!
Praise him with timbrel and dance;
    praise him with strings and pipe!
Praise him with sounding cymbals;
    praise him with loud clashing cymbals!
Let everything that breathes praise the Lord!
Praise the Lord!

It is clear enough that an editor or editorial committee has been at work here. All through the Psalter there are telltale signs of collecting and arranging.[2] A flood of new evidence, showing the extent and vitality of this work, has arrived in this century from the Psalms texts discovered in the Qumran caves, the popularly named Dead Sea Scrolls. This editorial work went on probably for a couple of centuries at least. All that editorial activity is evidence that prayer was getting a lot of attention in Israel. Providing the means by which people were taught and trained in prayer, responding to their God out of the specific actualities of their lives was high on the agenda, sharing top billing with the means for hearing the word itself. But the only part of this inspired editorial work that is unambiguously clear is its final edition where these concluding formulae are obvious and definitive. The prayers of Israel are grouped into entities and the groups ("books") are cleanly separated from one

---

2. Claus Westermann, *Praise and Lament in the Psalms,* trans. Keith R. Crim and Richard N. Soulen (Atlanta: John Knox Press, 1981), pp. 250-57; Gerald H. Wilson, *The Editing of the Hebrew Psalter* (Chico, CA: Scholars Press, 1985).

another. They are counted off. Finally it comes to an end. The fifth conclusion is a grand finale. We count five books; there are not going to be any more.

Why? It looks very much as if these prayers are arranged in five books to correspond to the first five books of the Bible, the Torah, contrasting and connecting the divine utterance (Torah) with the human answer (Psalms).[3] Christoph Barth calls this "the five-fold answer of the congregation to the word of God in the five books of Moses."[4] The *way* that something is said to us is often as important as *what* is said. Form can communicate as much as content. That is certainly true here. The care and art that were taken to fashion the fivefold shape of the Psalter invites a great deal more hermeneutical attention than is usually given to it. When pastors ponder and attend to this, we find that we are surprisingly well defended against at least one major enervating disease of prayer.

The Hebrews arranged their Scriptures in three large groups. Torah, the first five books of the Bible, was held to be God's primary speech. Everything that God wanted to say to us was said in Torah. Torah is the basic Bible; everything that follows in Scripture is derivative from it. The next major grouping, the Prophets (*nebiim*), presents the Torah in the changing historical circumstances across the centuries. The third grouping, the Writings (*kethubim*), gathers human responses to the divine word heard in the Torah and experienced in the Prophets. Sometimes these responses are argumentative as in Job, sometimes wise reflections as in Proverbs, but mostly they are prayer as in the Psalms. The Psalms dominate the Writings and

---

3. Artur Weiser, *The Old Testament: Its Formation and Development* (New York: Association Press, 1961), p. 286.

4. Christoph Barth, *Introduction to the Psalms*, trans. R. A. Wilson (New York: Charles Scribner's Sons, 1966), p. 4.

provide the major documentation for what it means to answer "out of the depths" the God who addresses his people. Athanasius, the fourth-century Egyptian theologian and bishop, pointed out their unique place in the Bible: most of Scripture speaks *to* us; the Psalms speak *for* us.[5]

The five-book arrangement of the Psalms is, then, strategic: for every word that God speaks *to* us there must be an answering word *from* us. No word of God can go unanswered. The word of God is not complete simply by being uttered; it must be answered. For the five books of God's creating/saving word to us there are five books of our believing/obeying word to God. Five is matched by five, like the fingers of two clasped hands.

But when we take the next step and begin to look for specific Psalm-answers to Torah-addresses we flounder. There is no apparent correspondence in subject matter between the two collections. The Torah progresses in chronological order from Adam to Moses. The Psalms are random and mixed, matching nothing specific in the Torah. Nor is there any other scheme of arrangement, such as thematic, in which various psalms are grouped together — psalms of praise, of lament, confessions, etc. Each of the five books contains all kinds of prayers grouped together rather haphazardly. There are some discernable subgroupings: Book II has a cluster of psalms that fit the historical circumstances of David's life; Book III has psalms ascribed to Asaph and Korah with connections in public worship; Book V has the remarkable sequence of psalms associated with temple pilgrimage. But all the same, in each of the five books every other kind of psalm is also included.

---

5. Quoted by Bernard W. Anderson, *Out of the Depths* (Philadelphia: Westminster Press, 1974), p. x.

It looks very much as if this internal nonarrangement is every bit as deliberate as the external five-book arrangement. And the reason is not far to seek: there are no stock catechism answers here for the simple reason that that is not the way communication takes place between living persons. The life that God calls into being in us is enormously various and infinitely complex. Rote responses are not adequate to the dazzling creativity of address that is put to us by God's word. What is required in us is not that we learn a specific answer to a specific address, but that we acquire facility in personal language that is accurately responsive to what we hear God say to us out of his word in Scripture and in Christ in our changing situations and various levels of faith. We need a vocabulary and syntax that is sufficiently personal and adequately wide-ranging to answer everything that God says from wherever we happen to hear it within every developing stage of our pilgrimage across the entire spectrum of our lives. So Psalm 1 is not the stock prayer-answer to Genesis 1, nor Psalm 2 to Genesis 2. What Psalm 1 does is introduce us to words and rhythms that will provide us with the means to answer Exodus 16 on one day and Deuteronomy 4 another. I read Numbers 22 one way when I was a seventeen-year-old student, another way as a forty-five-year-old pastor, and accurately both times. But my answers were accurate only when they spoke an obedience and faith issuing from a thoroughly personal and physical actual present. I need a language that is large enough to maintain continuities, supple enough to express nuances across a lifetime that brackets child and adult experiences, and courageous enough to explore all the countries of sin and salvation, mercy and grace, creation and covenant, anxiety and trust, unbelief and faith that comprise the continental human condition. The Psalms are this large, supple, and courageous language. John Calvin called the 150 Psalms an "anatomy of all the parts of the soul."[6] Everything that a person can possibly feel, experience, and say is brought into expression before God in the Psalms.

If we insist on being self-taught in prayer, our prayers, however eloquent, will be meagre. Inevitably they will be shaped on the one hand by whatever the congregational "market" demands, and restricted by our own little faith on the other. But pastors must live in the spacious country of the covenant and be on familiar terms with all the people and their dialects, know every nook and cranny in the landscape — not merely be informed *about* them as a tour guide might but at ease among them as one who has grown up there, playing in the mountains and working in the fields, falling in and out of love, getting hurt and getting well. It is no easy thing, venturing out of our cozy small-minded religious programs into a large-souled obedience, leaving the secure successes of our professionally defined lives and living by faith and love in prayer (which frequently involves failure and suffering). Where will we acquire a language that is adequate for these intensities? Where else but in the Psalms? For men and women who are called to leadership in the community of faith, apprenticeship in the Psalms is not an option; it is a mandate. Most of the church has agreed on this for most of its centuries. The Roman Catholic breviary, the Anglican Book of Common Prayer, and the Scottish Presbyterian Psalter, all "textbooks" for their respective clergy, are constructed from the Psalms. In his papal bull *Divine afflatu,* St. Pius X said: "The Psalms teach mankind, especially those vowed to a life of worship, how God is to be praised."[7] Too much is at stake here — the maturity of the

---

6. John Calvin, *Commentary on the Book of Psalms* (Grand Rapids: William B. Eerdmans, 1949), 1:xxxvii.

7. Michael Gasmer, O.P., *The Psalms, School of Spirituality* (St. Louis: B. Herder, 1961), p. 3.

word of God, the integrity of pastoral ministry, the health of worship — to permit pastors to pick and choose a curriculum of prayer as they are more or less inclined. We can as well permit a physician to concoct his medicines from the herbs and weeds in his backyard as allow a pastor to learn prayer from his or her own subjectivities. Prayer must not be fabricated out of emotional fragments or professional duties. Uninstructed and untrained, our prayers are something learned by tourists out of a foreign language phrase book: we give thanks at meals, repent of the grosser sins, bless the Rotary picnic, and ask for occasional guidance. Did we think prayer was merely a specialized and incidental language to get by on during those moments when we happened to pass through a few miles of religious country? But our entire lives are involved. We need fluency in the language of the country we live in. It is not enough merely to take notes on it for putting together the weekly report, which is a requirement of our job. We are required to be graduate students in this comprehensive grammar that provides all the parts of speech and complexities of syntax for "answering speech." Praying the Psalms, we find the fragments of soul and body, our own and all those with whom we have to do, spoken into adoration and love and faith. The Psalms, of course, are no special preserve of pastors. All who pray, Christians and Jews alike, find their praying "voice" in them — but for pastors, who are in a special place of responsibility to pray for others and to teach them to pray, it is a dereliction of duty to be ignorant of or negligent in them. St. Ambrose, using a different metaphor, called the Psalms "a sort of gymnasium for the use of all souls, a sort of stadium of virtue, where different sorts of exercise are set out before him, from which he can choose the best suited to train him to win his crown."[8]

---

8. Ambrose, *Discourses on the Psalms,* quoted in the reading for Thursday after Trinity, Book of Common Prayer.

• • •
• • •
• • •

Dr. Donald G. Miller once fashioned a kind of midrash on the five books of "Moses" that shows their implicit need to be answered with the passionate and personal intensities that are formed into prayer by the five books of "David."[9] The following summarizes his thought.

Genesis is the prenatal word of God. Everything in Genesis is embryonic. The seed of the word conceives a cosmos and a world and human beings — and a life of faith in Abraham. The beginnings are all here, but in the shadows, obscure in the womb. We know so little about the antediluvians and patriarchs — vast stretches of time and geography but only a few facts, a few stories. What is going to come of all this? The outlines of creation and covenant are definite, but the shapes are rudimentary, developing limbs and organs. We discern great energies gathering, an enormous hope swelling in the womb of Genesis.

Exodus is birth and infancy. The centuries-long Genesis pregnancy comes to term in the birth of the people of God. It is not an easy birth. There is a painful and arduous travail in Egypt, then the breaking of the Red Sea waters, and, marvelously and miraculously, the newborn on the far shore. A great celebrative joy issues from this birth: singing and dancing, praising and thanking. The infant people learn their first steps and receive their first instruction at the knee of Sinai: Do this, don't do that. It is a dangerous world in which they are launched, large with the goodness of God, perilous with the temptations to sin. Exodus shows this infant people, drawn out of the waters and taught their first toddling steps, as a people

---

9. To my knowledge this has not been published. I heard Dr. Miller present this in a Lenten Teaching Mission in 1978 at Calvary Baptist Church, Bel Air, Maryland.

at worship, attending and responding to the God who gave them birth and being.

Leviticus is childhood. The growing people learn the ABCs of life under the mercy and judgment of God. The great reality with which they have to do is God and their relation with him, a relation that is interrupted and tempered and interfered with in a thousand different ways. They learn the names of aspects of the faith relationship, and what to do when it goes awry. It is easier to learn geography, or physics, or grammar. But Leviticus makes it as easy as the subject allows by giving the instruction audiovisually: instead of abstract discussions about sin and grace, visible and tangible objects are set forth — a bowl of cereal, a red heifer, a scapegoat. Everything is presented in picture form (sacrifices) with a few simple actions that engage bodily participation (ritual). Leviticus is the McGuffy Reader for the children of God learning to read his word for the first time.

Numbers is adolescence. The people are reaching for adulthood, struggling through the awkwardness of the wilderness years. They rebel against authority, trying to arrive at who they are — no longer children, not yet experienced enough for life on their own. They are nostalgic for the secure and womblike Egyptian existence from which they were thrust into the austere realities of a life of faith. They are restless and impatient with the geriatric Mosaic establishment. They murmur and disobey; they grouse and grumble. Midway between their birth out of Egypt and their inheritance in Canaan they wallow in the no-man's-land of adolescent confusion.

Deuteronomy is adulthood. Finally, the people are grown up in God. They have matured into a life of faith and are capable of receiving the promised land inheritance and of living responsibly in it. They are well educated, superbly trained, extensively tested. God is about to entrust them with what he has prepared for them. Moses, about to pass from the scene after which they will be on their own, gathers up in sermonic form all that they have experienced together in their forty wilderness years, all that God has revealed to them of his will and ways, all the grave and glorious matters of a life of faith. At the boundary between wilderness and promised land, Moses brings them to attention in a magnificent act of worship — he presents them before God, presents God before them — and blesses them. S. R. Driver, in his searching study of Deuteronomy, concluded that the single word that is both characteristic and definitive in that book is "love."[10] That is powerfully significant, for we are not capable of love until we are adult (or, to put it differently, when we are capable of love we are adults). Love integrates all that develops in us as we grow from infancy through childhood and adolescence and then presents that wholeness for intimate and faithful personal relationships, with each other and with God.

∴∴

Professor Miller's "midrash" provides a perspective for looking at the fivefold Torah as the word of God that comprehensively calls us into being, from new birth to mature love, and therefore requires a matching comprehensiveness in our responses in the fivefold Psalter. All prayer is restored to its proper context in the word of God. The word of God does not work impersonally or mechanically, stamping the divine will into dumb matter; *persons* are brought into being, *lives* are shaped by grace and in love. When persons are at issue, language is in the fore, and language at its finest is conversation, address and response,

---

10. S. R. Driver, *A Critical and Exegetical Commentary on Deuteronomy* (New York: Charles Scribner's Sons, 1895), pp. xxvii-xxxiv.

question and answer. The life of faith is not *done to* us but *developed in* us by commanding and blessing words that are completed in words of obedient assent and willing praise. All the parts of our lives and all the parts of our history are addressed by God and then answered by us.[11] The all-encompassing, everything-penetrating word of God constitutes the environment in which we live. One of the primary pastoral tasks is to make sure that not a single word in it drifts off into the abstractly impersonal or congeals into the merely informational. It is *all* personal address. Pastoral work means staying awake and keeping others awake to this language and giving answer to every word of it. Not all at once, of course, but all the time, for nothing in our lives escapes the creative and saving word of God that invites answers in the faith and obedience language of prayer.

---

11. This point is well made by Mascall:

Now the intercourse of personal beings, even on the finite and created level, is characteristically one of conversation, of the mutual communication of thought and knowledge; this is why language plays such an important part in human society. And even when two human beings achieve such a degree of union that at the points of its highest realization, language gives way to silence, the element of communication, indeed of self-communication, so far from vanishing remains and is enhanced. Indeed, if I have been right in asserting that the essence of knowledge is that the knower in a mysterious way, "ontentionally" as the Thomists say, *becomes* the object known, it is impossible to conceive even the lowest and most uncommitted modes of human communication as leaving the knower and the known entirely external to each other. All the more then, when we consider the possibility of God revealing himself to man, is it impossible to think of God as making a purely external impact upon man or as simply offering him items of information.

E. L. Mascall, *The Openness of Being* (Philadelphia: Westminster Press, 1971), pp. 148-49.

III

Prayer Time

I T CAME as a surprise, when I entered upon my pastoral vocation, that on any day of the week an astonishing number of people, in and out of my congregation, wanted me to do something for them. I was expecting a rather quiet life of study and prayer, visitation of the infirm and the dying, with occasional interruptions at times of crisis. I had concluded from reading the sociologists that religion was low on the agenda of people's concerns these days and that except for those infrequent times when family pressure or community protocol required my presence people would treat me with benign neglect. For years I had heard quips with variations on the theme of the pastor who works only one day a week, and supposed that there must be some basis in reality for the long life of the taunt. (My favorite is of the Scottish pastor who was "invisible six days a week and incomprehensible the seventh.") Each week I walk home after conducting Sunday worship and get a personalized version of this as my neighbor, puttering in his yard, greets me with the jibe, spoken as if he had just thought it up, "Finished for another week, huh? Sure must be nice." I am congenial in my answer: "Yup, sure is." Inwardly, I am not so good-natured: I mentally write out a description of my work-week that I will later take over and present to him, documenting evidence that will reassure him that I am not a parasite on the system, endangering the property values of the neighborhood with my indolence. He will register total shock and fumble out an apology. But after a long shower and some expertly phrased compliments from my wife on the prophetic originality of the morning sermon the sting is out of his barbs and I shelve my defense for another week.

Initially, the daily surprise of the demand-filled day was welcome. It continued to be welcome for several years. It is nice to be needed. More than nice: it is downright flattering. Nearly all the requests for my pastoral attention and presence were couched in the rhetoric of urgency. That, combined with the presumed connection in whatever I was doing with God or Eternity or Holiness, meant that even trivial actions got dressed out into affairs of Importance. It was also nice to know that the sociologists were wrong.

The edge began to wear off of the flattery when I realized that among the considerable demands on my time not one demanded that I practice a life of prayer. And yet prayer was at the very heart of the vocation I had entered. I was entrusted with nurturing a living conversation with the people with whom I was living and the living God. I had not knowingly signed on as a schoolmaster, pedantically instructing reluctant children in the three R's of God, but had accepted a call to be a companion to people on a pilgrimage that involved practicing the presence of God. I had not agreed to be a moral errand-boy doing the good deeds in congregation and community that the others in the press of their serious business of getting on in the world didn't have time for themselves, but had accepted responsibility for personally listening to and answering the word of God and guiding others into a similar listening and answering that constitute our mature humanity.

Busyness, of course, is not peculiar to the pastoral life; it is endemic to our culture. One critic complained that "most of us have taxi-meters for brains, ticking away, translating time and space into money."[1] But there are pastoral dimensions that require something other than a good scolding. We need a strategy that takes into account the daily dilemma of living between these two sets of demands that seem to cancel each other out, a strategy that accepts both sets without favoring one over the other. The first set of demands is that we respond with compassionate attentiveness to the demands of the people around us, demands that refuse to stay within the confines of regular hours and always exceed our capacity to meet them all. These demands often mask deep spiritual hungers and cannot be dismissed with a bromide or delegated to a committee. The lives of people hang by a thread on some of these demands and require discerning intelligence. The second set of demands is that we respond with reverent prayer to the demand of God for our attention, to listen to him, to take him seriously in the actual circumstances of this calendar day, at this street address, and not bluff our way through by adopting a professionalized role. This is a kind of attentiveness that we know from instruction and experience can be entered into only slowly and deliberately. There is a large, leisurely center to existence where God must be deeply pondered, lovingly believed. This demand is not for prayer-on-the-run or for prayer-on-request. It means entering realms of spirit where wonder and adoration have space to develop, where play and delight have time to flourish. Is this possible for pastors who have this other set before them daily? Is not this something for monks and nuns in monasteries, for hermits in

---

1. Wayne Oates, *Workaholics, Making Laziness Work for You* (Garden City, NY: Doubleday & Co., 1978), p. 59.

desert places, and for a few noble souls who manage to live beyond the limitations of our common mortality?

It is possible for pastors. Because there is a biblical provision for it, pastors across the centuries were able to integrate the two sets of demands instead of experiencing them, angrily and guiltily, as a dilemma. The name for it is *sabbath*. The single act of keeping a sabbath does more than anything else to train pastors in the rhythm of action and response so that the two sets of demands are experienced synchronically instead of violently.

An accurate understanding of sabbath is prerequisite to its practice: it must be understood biblically, not culturally. A widespread misunderstanding of sabbath trivializes it by designating it "a day off." Sabbath is not a day off and it is inexcusable that pastors, learned in Scripture and guardians of the sacred practices, should so misname it. "A day off" is a bastard sabbath. Days off are not without benefits, to be sure, but sabbaths they are not. Pastors are often persuaded by wives, husbands, children, and psychiatrists to interrupt their obsessive-compulsive seven-day week by taking a day off. They are often pleased with the results: they get more done on the six days than they used to on seven. Mind and body are not constructed for perpetual motion. Mental and physical health improve markedly with a day off. We feel better. Efficiency sharpens. Relationships improve. However beneficial, this is not a true sabbath but a secularized sabbath. The motivation is utilitarian: the day off is at the service of the six working days. The purpose is to restore strength, increase motivation, reward effort, and keep performance incentives high. It just so happens that the side effects of shored-up family harmony and improved mental health are also attractive. The nearly wholesale substitution among pastors of a day off for a sabbath is one more sign of an abandoned vocational identity. (A related misnaming replaces "pastor's study" with "office," thereby further secularizing perceptions of pastoral work. How many pastors no longer come to their desks as places for learning but as operation centers for organizing projects? The change of vocabulary is not harmless. Words have ways of shaping us. If we walk into a room labeled "office" often enough we end up doing office work. First we change the word, then the word changes us.)

∴ ∴

Sabbath means quit. Stop. Take a break. Cool it. The word itself has nothing devout or holy in it. It is a word about time, denoting our nonuse of it, what we usually call *wasting* time.

The biblical context for understanding sabbath is the Genesis week. Sabbath is the seventh and final day in which "God rested [*shabath*] from all his work which he had done" (Gen. 2:3). We reenter that sequence of days in which God spoke energy and matter into existence, and repeatedly come upon the refrain, "And there was evening and there was morning, one day. . . . And there was evening and there was morning, a second day. . . . And there was evening and there was morning" — on and on, six times.

This is the Hebrew way of understanding *day;* it is not ours. American days, most of them anyway, begin with an alarm clock ripping the predawn darkness, and they close, not with evening, but several hours past that, when we turn off the electric lights. In conventional references to *day* we do not include the night hours except for the two or three that we steal from either end to give us more time to work. Because our definition of *day* is so different, we have to make an imaginative effort to understand the Hebrew phrase *evening and morning, one day.* More than idiomatic speech is involved here; there is a sense of rhythm. Day is the basic unit of God's creative work; evening is the beginning of that day. It is the onset of God speaking light, stars, earth, vegetation, animals, man, woman into being. But it is also the time when we quit our activity and go to sleep. When it is evening "I lay me down to sleep and pray the Lord my soul to keep" and drift off into unconsciousness for the next six or eight or ten hours, a state in which I am absolutely nonproductive and have no cash value.

Then I wake up, rested, jump out of bed full of energy, grab a cup of coffee, and rush out the door to get things started. The first thing I discover (a great blow to the ego) is that everything was started hours ago. All the important things got underway while I was fast asleep. When I dash into the work-day, I walk into an operation that is half over already. I enter into work in which the basic plan is already established, the assignments given, the operations in motion.

Sometimes, still in a stupor, I blunder into the middle of something that is nearly done, and go to work thinking that I am starting it. But when I do I interfere with what is already far along on its way to completion. My sincere intentions and cheerful whistle while I work make it no less a blunder and an aggravation. The sensible thing is to ask, "Where do I fit? Where do you need an extra hand? What still needs to be done?"

The Hebrew evening/morning sequence conditions us to the rhythms of grace. We go to sleep, and God begins his work. As we sleep he develops his covenant. We wake and are called out to participate in God's creative action. We respond in faith, in work. But always grace is previous. Grace is primary. We wake into a world we didn't make, into a salvation we didn't earn. Evening: God begins, without our help, his creative day. Morning: God calls us to enjoy and share and develop the work he initiated. Creation and covenant are sheer grace and there to greet us every morning. George MacDonald once wrote that sleep is God's contrivance for giving us the help he cannot get into us when we are awake.

We read and reread these opening pages of Genesis, along with certain sequences of Psalms, and recover these deep, elemental rhythms, internalizing the reality in which the strong, initial pulse is God's creating/saving word, God's providential/sustaining presence, God's grace.

As this biblical genesis rhythm works in me, I also discover something else: when I quit my day's work, nothing essential stops. I prepare for sleep not with a feeling of exhausted frustration because there is so much yet undone and unfinished, but with expectancy. The day is about to begin! God's genesis words are about to be spoken again. During the hours of my sleep, how will he prepare to use my obedience, service, and speech when morning breaks? I go to sleep to get out of the way for awhile. I get into the rhythm of salvation. While we sleep, great and marvelous things, far beyond our capacities to invent or engineer, are in process — the moon marking the seasons, the lion roaring for its prey, the earthworms aerating the earth, the stars turning in their courses, the proteins repairing our muscles, our dreaming brains restoring a deeper sanity beneath the gossip and scheming of our waking hours. Our work settles into the context of God's work. Human effort is honored and respected not as a thing in itself but by its integration into the rhythms of grace and blessing.

We experience this grace with our bodies before we apprehend it with our minds. We are attending to a matter of physical/spiritual *technology* — not ideas, not doctrines, not virtues. We are getting our bodies into a genesis rhythm.

Sabbath extrapolates this basic, daily rhythm into the larger context of the month. The turning of the earth on its axis gives us the basic two-beat rhythm, evening/morning. The moon in its orbit introduces another rhythm, the twenty-eight-day month, marked by four phases of seven days each. It is this larger rhythm, the rhythm of the seventh day, that we are commanded to observe. Sabbath-keeping presumes the daily rhythm, evening/morning. We can hardly avoid stopping our work each night as fatigue and sleep overtake us. But we can avoid stopping work on the seventh day, especially if things are gaining momentum. Keeping the weekly rhythm requires deliberate action. Sabbath-keeping often feels like an interruption, an interference with our routines. It challenges assumptions we gradually build up that our daily work is indispensable in making the world go. And then we find that it is not an interruption but a more spacious rhythmic measure that confirms and extends the basic beat. Every seventh day a deeper note is struck — an enormous gong whose deep sounds reverberate under and over and around the daily timpani percussions of evening/morning, evening/morning, evening/morning: creation honored and contemplated, redemption remembered and shared.

In the two biblical versions of the sabbath commandment, the commands are identical but the supporting reasons differ. The Exodus reason is that we are to keep a sabbath because God kept it (Exod. 20:8-11). God did his work in six days and then rested. If God sets apart one day to rest, we can too. There are some things that can be accomplished, even by God, only in a state of rest. The work/rest rhythm is built into the very structure of God's interpenetration of reality. The precedent to quit doing and simply *be* is divine. Sabbath-keeping is commanded so that we internalize the being that matures out of doing.

The Deuteronomy reason for Sabbath-keeping is that our ancestors in Egypt went four hundred years without a vacation (Deut. 5:15). Never a day off. The consequence: they were no longer considered persons but slaves. Hands. Work units. Not persons created in the image of God but equipment for making bricks and building pyramids. Humanity was defaced.

Lest any of us do that to our neighbor or husband or wife or child or employee, we are commanded to keep a sabbath. The moment we begin to see others in terms of what they can *do* rather than who they *are*, we mutilate humanity and violate community. It is no use claiming "I don't need to rest this week and therefore will not keep a sabbath" — our lives are so interconnected that we inevitably involve others in our work whether we intend it or not. Sabbath-keeping is elemental kindness. Sabbath-keeping is commanded to preserve the image of God in our neighbors so that we see them as they are, not as we need them or want them.

It is of interest to note that the truth and necessity of seven of the ten commandments are obvious and need no clarification. The second commandment is difficult to keep and so is backed up by a warning. The fifth commandment is fatiguing to keep and so gets the support of a promise. But the fourth commandment appears neither necessary nor logical, and so reasons are given for it. It is one of the ironies of history that our age, which prides itself on its appeal to reason, is most disregarding of the one commandment that is supported by reason — a double reason actually, one historical, the other theological.

Every profession has sins to which it is especially liable. I haven't looked closely into the sins that endanger physicians and lawyers, woodworkers and potters, but I have had my eye out for the snare of the fowler from which pastors need daily deliverance: it is the sin of reversing the rhythms. Instead of grace/work we make it work/grace. Instead of working in a world in which God calls everything into being with his word and redeems his people with an outstretched arm, we rearrange it as a world in which we preach the mighty word of God and in afterthought ask him to bless our speaking; a world in which we stretch out our mighty arms to help the oppressed and open our hands to assist the needy and desperately petition God to take care of those we miss.

And that, of course, is why so few pastors keep a sabbath: we have reversed the rhythms. How can we quit work for a day when we have reversed the rhythms? How can we quit work for a day when we have been commanded to redeem the time? How can we shut up when we have fire in our mouth? How can we do nothing for a whole day when we have been told on high authority to be urgent in season and out of season, and there is never a season in which the calls for help do not exceed our capacity to meet them? But that is also why the sabbath is *commanded* and not just *suggested*, for nothing less than a command has the power to intervene in the vicious, accelerating, self-perpetuating cycle of faithless and graceless busyness, the only part of which we are conscious being our good intentions.

It is diagnostically significant that of all the commandments not one is treated with such contemptuous disregard by pastors as this one. We are capable of preaching good sermons on it to our parishioners, and take great care to provide them a sabbath of good worship and holy leisure. But we exempt ourselves. Curious. Not many of us preach vigorously on the seventh commandment and then pursue lives of active adultery. Not many of us preach eloquently on the second commandment and then moonlight by selling plastic fertility goddesses in the narthex. But we conscientiously catechize our people on the fifth commandment and without a blush flaunt our workaholic sabbath-breaking as evidence of an extraordinary piety.

Sabbath: Uncluttered time and space to distance ourselves

from the frenzy of our own activities so we can see what God has been and is doing. If we do not regularly quit work for one day a week we take ourselves far too seriously. The moral sweat pouring off our brows blinds us to the primal action of God in and around us.

Sabbath-keeping: Quieting the internal noise so we hear the still small voice of our Lord. Removing the distractions of pride so we discern the presence of Christ ". . . in ten thousand places, / Lovely in limbs, and lovely in eyes not his / To the Father through the features of men's faces."[2]

Sabbath: Uncluttered time and space to detach ourselves from the people around us so that they have a chance to deal with God without our poking around and kibitzing. They need to be free from depending on us. They need to be free from our guidance that always tends toward manipulation.

Sabbath-keeping: Separating ourselves from the people who are clinging to us, from the routines to which we are clinging for our identity, and offering them all up to God in praise.

None of us have trouble with this theologically. We are compellingly articulate on the subject in our pulpits. Our theology is orthodox and biblical in these matters. It is not our theology that is deficient, but our technology — sabbath-keeping is not a matter of belief but of using a tool (time), not an exercise of heart and mind but of the body. Sabbath-keeping is not devout thoughts or heart praise but simply removing our bodies from circulation one day a week.

We are, most of us, Augustinians in our pulpits. We preach the sovereignty of our Lord, the primacy of grace, the glory of God: "By grace are ye saved. . . . Not of works, lest any man

---

2. Gerard Manley Hopkins, "As Kingfishers Catch Fire," in *Poems and Prose of Gerard Manley Hopkins,* ed. W. H. Gardner (Baltimore: Penguin Books, 1953), p. 51.

should boast" (Eph. 2:8-9, KJV). But the minute we leave our pulpits we are Pelagians. In our committee meetings and our planning sessions, in our obsessive attempts to meet the expectations of people, in our anxiety to please, in our hurry to cover all the bases, we practice a theology that puts our good will at the foundation of life and urges moral effort as the primary element in pleasing God.

The dogma produces the behavior characteristic of the North American pastor: if things aren't good enough, they will improve if I work a little harder and get others to work harder. Add a committee here, recruit some more volunteers there, squeeze a couple of hours more into the workday.

Pelagius was an unlikely heretic; Augustine an unlikely saint. By all accounts Pelagius was urbane, courteous, convincing. Everyone seems to have liked him immensely. Augustine squandered away his youth in immorality, had some kind of Freudian thing with his mother, and made a lot of enemies. But all our theological and pastoral masters agree that Augustine started from God's grace and therefore had it right, and Pelagius started from human effort and therefore got it wrong. If we were as Augustinian out of the pulpit as we are in it, we would have no difficulty keeping sabbath. How did it happen that Pelagius became our master?

Our closet Pelagianism will not get us excommunicated or burned at the stake, but it cripples our pastoral work severely, and while that is not personally painful, it is catastrophic to the church's wholeness and health.

$$\bullet \ \bullet \ \bullet$$
$$\bullet \ \bullet \ \bullet$$
$$\bullet \ \bullet \ \bullet$$

The two biblical reasons for sabbath-keeping develop into parallel sabbath activities of praying and playing. The Exodus reason directs us to the contemplation of God, which becomes prayer. The Deuteronomy reason directs us to social leisure, which becomes play. Praying and playing are deeply congruent with each other and have extensive inner connections, noted and commented upon by a wide range of philosophers and theologians.[3] John Calvin filled his sabbath with both. His reputation for humorless austerity doesn't prepare us for the facts: he led his congregation in prayers in the morning and in the afternoon went among the people of Geneva and played skittles.[4] In our own time the poet W. H. Auden was alarmed that we are losing two of our most precious qualities, the ability to laugh heartily and the ability to pray, and he pleaded on behalf of a sane world for better prayer and better play.[5]

Psalm 92 is the one biblical Psalm specifically assigned to the sabbath. Its opening lines put the normative sabbath actions in parallel:

> It is good to give thanks to Yahweh,
> to play in honour of your name, Most High.
> (92:1, Jerusalem Bible)

What is it like to pray? To play? Puritan sabbaths that eliminated play were a disaster. Secular sabbaths that eliminate prayer are worse. Sabbath-keeping involves both playing and praying. The activities are alike enough to share the same day and different enough to require each other for a complementary wholeness. But combining them is not easy. It is easier to specialize in an "Exodus sabbath" or a "Deuteronomy sabbath." George Sheehan once wrote that "man playing is almost as

---

3. Hugo Rahner, *Man at Play* (New York: Herder and Herder, 1972).

4. Tilden Edwards, *Sabbath Time* (New York: Seabury Press, 1982), p. 20.

5. May Sarton, *Journal of a Solitude* (New York: W. W. Norton & Co., 1973), p. 98.

difficult a subject as man praying."[6] But children do both all the time, showing that playing and praying are not alien habits that we have to acquire but rather the recovery of something deeply essential within us that we "have loved long since and lost awhile" (Newman).

A Rembrandt etching shows Jesus teaching a group of adults who are before him rapt and reverent. Off to the side a child is absorbed in playing with a string and top. Rembrandt doesn't tell us what Jesus is saying. I think he is teaching us how to pray. The child is showing us how to play. (A twenty-year-old memory carries a similar juxtaposition. I opened my eyes after leading my congregation in intercessory prayers and saw my infant son crawling across the center of the sanctuary in pursuit of a ball he was playing with while I and the congregation were praying. My initial response was of embarrassment. I later repented. Was his playing less to the glory of God than our praying?)

Psalm 92 sets praying and playing in tandem and then elaborates the parallel actions with three metaphors, providing us with a triptych of sabbath-keeping.

The first metaphor is musical: we pray and play "to the music of the zither and lyre, to the rippling of the harp" (v. 3, JB). Playing and praying are like the musicians' art that combines discipline with delight. Music quickens something deep within us. Our bodies assimilate the sound and rhythm and experience aliveness. Melody and harmony draw us over the boundary of the tuneless grunts and groans of daily discourse, the demands and complaints that fence us into the corral of self. When played well, musical performance seems effortless, yet behind the easy spontaneity is an immense discipline. This

---

6. George Sheehan, *On Running* (Mountain View, CA: World Publications, 1975), p. 196.

discipline, while arduous, is not onerous, but is the accepted means for taking us beyond our plodding exterior selves into perceptions and aspirations that stretch us into beauty. And any time we are beyond ourselves, by whatever means, we are closer to God. Surely it is significant that nearly all the prayers in the Psalter carry evidence within them of being played musically. Karl Barth once declared that the music of Mozart led him "to the threshold of a world which in sunlight and storm, by day and by night, is a good and ordered world."[7]

A clever and learned atheist showed up in ancient Rome, badgering the people with his arguments and reasoning that there was no God, no purpose, no meaning, and that therefore anything was permitted. He picked on a rude shepherd in the town square as a foil for his arguments, thinking to make sport of him before the spectators. He cut him up with his razor logic, befuddled him with his narcotic eloquence. He concluded with a flourish: "What do you say to *that!*" The shepherd took out his flute and played a lively tune. Within minutes all the people in the square were dancing for joy.

A second metaphor is animal: praying and playing are like the ox's wildness: "you raise my horn as if I were a wild ox" (v. 10, JB). Animal wildness is unfettered exuberance. We are delighted when we see animals in their natural environments — leaping, soaring, prancing. A golden eagle plummets to its prey; a grizzly bear carelessly rips through alpine turf, lunching on tubers; a white-tailed deer vaults a stream. Praying and playing are like that: undomesticated. We shed poses and masks. We become unself-conscious. We *are.*

Erik Erikson expounds on this:

---

7. Karl Barth, "A Letter of Thanks to Mozart," in *Wolfgang Amadeus Mozart,* trans. Clarence K. Pott (Grand Rapids: William B. Eerdmans, 1986), p. 22.

Of all the formulations of play, the briefest and the best is to be found in Plato's *Laws*. He sees the model of true playfulness in the need of all young creatures, animal and human, to leap. To truly leap, you must learn how to use the ground as a springboard, and how to land resiliently and safely. It means to test the leeway allowed by given limits; to outdo and yet not escape gravity. Thus, wherever playfulness prevails, there is always a surprising element, surpassing mere repetition or habituation, and at best suggesting some virgin chance conquered, some divine leeway shared.[8]

Substitute the word *pray* for *play* in that passage; it reads the same.

The third metaphor is sylvan: persons who pray and play

> . . . flourish like palm trees
> and grow as tall as the cedars of Lebanon.
> Planted in the house of Yahweh,
> they will flourish in the courts of our God,
> still bearing fruit in old age,
> still remaining fresh and green.
>
> (Vv. 12-14, JB)

Praying and playing share this quality: they develop and mature with age, they don't go into decline. Prayerfulness and playfulness reverse the deadening effects of sin-determined lives. They are life-enhancing, not life-diminishing. They infuse vitalities, counteracting fatigue. They renew us, they do not wear us out. Playing and praying counter boredom, reduce anxieties, push, pull, direct, prod us into the fullness of our humanity by getting body and spirit in touch and friendly with each other. "Man," wrote Schiller, "only plays when in

---

8. Erik Erikson, *Toys and Reasons* (New York: W. W. Norton, 1977), p. 17.

the full meaning of the word he is a man, and he is only completely a man when he plays."[9]

Johann Huizinga wrote a long and learned book, *Homo Ludens,* showing that culture is healthy only when it plays.[10] Play is a distinctive mode of activity for humans. When we repress or neglect play we dehumanize culture. Huizinga writes to warn. As our civilization has advanced, it has lost touch with the distinctively human, and so while we show off a breathtakingly wealthy technology, our collective humanity has dipped well below the poverty level. We are less ourselves. Unpraying and unplaying, we deteriorate into skid-row consumers, life meagre with mere *getting.* Pastors must be in the avant garde of sabbath-keepers, reforesting our land, so savagely denuded by the humorless bulldozers, with playgrounds, prayergrounds.

⋮ ⋮ ⋮

These three metaphors combine to characterize sabbath-keeping with a kind of audacious, necessity-defying insouciance. The context brings this out: the three play/pray metaphors are developed in a psalm that is centrally concerned with the enormous fact of evil. Bounded on one side by prayerful play and on the other with playful prayer, the psalm center has this:

> Great are your achievements, Yahweh,
> immensely deep your thoughts!
> Stupid men are not aware of this,
> fools can never appreciate it.
> The wicked may sprout as thick as weeds
> and every evil-doer flourish,

9. Quoted in Norman Brown, *Life against Death* (Middletown, CT: Wesleyan University Press, 1959), p. 33.

10. Johann Huizinga, *Homo Ludens* (Boston: Beacon Press, 1955).

but only to be everlastingly destroyed,
whereas you are supreme for ever.
See how your enemies perish,
how all evil men are routed.

(Ps. 92:5-9, JB)

This sabbath-psalmist is not off smelling the flowers, dreamily detached from the awful plight of the people. He is appalled that the wicked are "thick as weeds." He is dismayed that evil-doers flourish. But he goes ahead and keeps a sabbath of praying and playing. Pastors who keep a weekly sabbath know full well the ruined state of the world. They play and pray anyway — not because they are heartlessly selfish or trivially giddy, but because they are convinced that these practices are God's will not only for them but also for the battered world. There is a devil-may-care recklessness that sets the day aside for praying and playing despite compelling pressure to do something practical — and then discovers that this was the most practical thing of all to do.

The technology of sabbath-keeping is not complex. We simply select a day of the week (Paul seemed to think any day would do as well as any other; Rom. 14:5-6) and quit our work.

Having selected the day we need also to protect it, for our workday instincts and habits will not serve us well. It is not a day when we do anything useful. It is not a day that proves its worth, justifies itself. Entering into empty, nonfunctional time is difficult and needs protection, for we have been taught that time is money.

Our secularized age is so fragmented that no consensus in the details of sabbath-keeping is possible. We cannot prescribe a practice for each other. But lest the command dissolve into a fog of good intentions, I will risk autobiography. The risk is that someone will try to imitate the details of my practice, or (more likely) will say, "That's sure dumb; I don't see the point of that" and dismiss the whole business on the basis of my inept practice. I excuse my example giving with Thoreau's precedent: "I should not talk so much about myself if there were anybody else whom I knew as well. Unfortunately, I am confined to this theme by the narrowness of my experience."

Monday is my sabbath. Nothing is scheduled for Mondays. If there are emergencies I respond, but there are surprisingly few. My wife joins me in observing the day. We make a lunch, put it in a daypack, take our binoculars, and drive anywhere from fifteen minutes to an hour away, to a trailhead along a river or into the mountains. Before we begin our hike my wife reads a psalm and prays. After that prayer there is no more talking — we enter into a silence that will continue for the next two or three hours, until we stop for lunch.

We walk leisurely, emptying ourselves, opening ourselves to what is there: fern shapes, flower fragrance, birdsong, granite outcropping, oaks and sycamores, rain, snow, sleet, wind. We have clothes for all weather and so never cancel our sabbath-keeping for reasons of weather any more than our Sunday church-going — and for the same reason: we need our sabbath just as much as our parishioners need theirs. When the sun or our stomachs tell us it is lunchtime, we break the silence with a prayer of blessing for the sandwiches and fruit, the river and the forest. We are free to talk now, sharing bird sightings, thoughts, observations, ideas — however much or little we are inclined. We return home in the middle or late afternoon, putter, do odd jobs, read. After supper I usually write family letters. That's it. No Sinai thunder. No Damascus Road illuminations. No Patmos visions. A day set apart for solitude and silence. Not-doing. Being-there. The sanctification of time.

We don't have any rules for preserving the sanctity of the day, only the commitment that it be set apart for being, not using. Not a day to get anything done but a day to watch and be responsive to what God has done.

But we have help. Sabbath-keeping cannot be carried out as a private enterprise. We need our congregation's help. They need our help to keep their sabbath; we need their help to keep ours. From time to time I say something like this to my elders and deacons: "The great reality we are involved in as people and pastor is God. Most of the people around us don't know that, and couldn't care less. One of the ways God has provided for us to stay aware of and responsive to him as the determining and centering reality of our lives in a world that doesn't care about it is by sabbath-keeping. At regular intervals we all need to quit *our* work and contemplate *his,* quit talking to each other and listen to *him.* God knows we need this and has given us a means in sabbath — a day for praying and playing, simply enjoying what he is. One of my tasks is to lead you in the celebrative keeping of sabbath each Sunday. But that is not a sabbath for me. I wake up on Sunday morning with the adrenalin flowing. It is a workday for me. Monday is my sabbath, and I need your help to observe it. I need your prayers; I need your cooperation in not involving me in administration or consultation; I need your admonitions if you see me care-lessly letting other things interfere with it. Pastors need pastors too. One of the ways you can be my pastor is to help me keep a weekly sabbath that God commanded."

And they do it. They help. I don't think there are many congregations who would not help us do it if they knew we were committed to it and needed their help to carry it out.

My wife has been keeping, off and on, a sabbath journal for the fourteen years that we have been doing this. The journal is labeled "Emmaus Walks." You wouldn't be greatly impressed, I think, if you read the sporadic entries. Bird lists, wildflowers in bloom, snatches of conversation, brief notes on the weather. But the spareness records a fullness, a presence. For sabbath-keeping is not primarily something we do, but what we don't do.

We got the phrase "Emmaus Walks" in conversation with Douglas V. Steere, who told us the story of an old Lutheran retreat master he once knew, very Prussian, whose speech was thick with German gutterals. He specialized in men's retreats. As the men would come into the lodge, he would make them open their suitcases, from which he would confiscate all the whiskey. Then he would pair them up and send them off on what he called *ee-mouse* walks. Steere told us that for a long time he wondered what *ee-mouse* walks were, and then realized one day that the old Prussian drillmaster was sending his men out on Emmaus walks: two disciples walking and talking together and Jesus, unrecognized, with them. But afterward they knew: "Did not our hearts burn within us while he talked to us on the road, while he opened to us the scriptures?" (Luke 24:32). It is the kind of unobtrusive alteration in perception and prayer that happens quietly but cumulatively in the practice of sabbath-keeping. We get the rhythms right. And with the rhythms right, we realize that without directly intending it, we have time to pray.

SCRIPTURE

IV

Turning Eyes into Ears

I T IS AN immense irony when the very practice of our work results in abandoning our work. In the course of doing our work we leave our work. But in reading, teaching, and preaching the Scriptures it happens: we cease to *listen* to the Scriptures and thereby undermine the intent of having Scripture in the first place.

Reading Scripture is not the same as listening to God. To do one is not necessarily to do the other. But they are often assumed to be the same thing. Pastors, who spend more of their time reading the Scriptures than most Christians do (not because of their devoutness but because of their job), make this unwarranted assumption with alarming frequency.

This happens so commonly and so insidiously that we have to be analytically alert to the ways in which listening to the word of God slides off into reading about the word of God, and then energetically recover an open ear.

The Christian's interest in Scripture has always been in hearing God speak, not in analyzing moral memos. The common practice is to nurture a listening disposition — the involving ear rather than the distancing eye — hoping to become passionate hearers of the word rather than cool readers of the page. But it is just this quality of zestful passion to *listen* to Scripture that diminishes, even to the point of disappearance, in the course of pastoral work. When it does, one of the essential angles that defines and gives precision to our work is gone. This does not happen because pastors repudiate or neglect Scripture: it takes place in the very act of *reading* Scripture. The reading itself is responsible for the deadly work.

Listening and reading are not the same thing. They involve different senses. In listening we use our ears; in reading we use our eyes. We listen to the sound of a voice; we read marks on paper. These differences are significant and have profound consequences. Listening is an interpersonal act; it involves two or more people in fairly close proximity. Reading involves one person with a book written by someone who can be miles away or centuries dead, or both. The listener is required to be attentive to the speaker and is more or less at the speaker's mercy. For the reader it is quite different, since the book is at the reader's mercy. It may be carried around from place to place, opened or shut at whim, read or not read. When I read a book the book does not know if I am paying attention or not; when I listen to a person the person knows very well whether I am paying attention or not. In listening, another initiates the process; when I read I initiate the process. In reading I open the book and attend to the words. I can read by myself; I cannot listen by myself. In listening the speaker is in charge; in reading the reader is in charge.

Many people much prefer reading over listening. It is less demanding emotionally and can be arranged to suit personal convenience. The stereotype is the husband buried in the morning newspaper at breakfast, preferring to read a news agency report of the latest scandal in a European government, the scores of yesterday's athletic contests, and the opinions of a couple of columnists whom he will never meet rather than listen to the voice of the person who has just shared his bed, poured his coffee, and fried his eggs, even though listening to that live voice promises love and hope, emotional depth and intellectual exploration far in excess of what he can gather informationally from *The New York Times, The Wall Street Journal,* and *The Christian Science Monitor* put together. In the voice of this living person he has access to a colorful history, an incredibly complex emotional system, and never-before-heard combinations of words that can surprise, startle, move, gladden, or anger him — any of which would seem to be more attractive to an alive human being than getting some information, none or little of which will make any impact on the living of that day. Reading does not, as such, increase our capacity to listen. In some cases it interferes with it.

The intent in reading Scripture, among people of faith, is to extend the range of our listening to the God who reveals himself in word, to become acquainted with the ways in which he has spoken in various times and places, along with the ways in which people respond when he speaks. The Christian conviction is that God speaks reality into being — creation into shape, salvation into action. It is also a Christian conviction that *we* are *that* which is spoken into a creation shape and a salvation action. We are what happens when the word is spoken. So we listen in order to find out what is going on — in *us*. Ezra Pound's H. Selwyn Mauberly expresses the zest of this kind of reader/listener: "Tell it to me, all of it, I guzzle with outstretched ears!"[1]

But what if the reading never arrives at listening? And what if the persons entrusted by these faith communities to

---

1. Ezra Pound, "Hugh Selwyn Mauberly," in *Selected Poems* (London: Faber & Faber, 1928), pp. 173-87.

direct its listening to the word of God in Scripture through public readings, by preaching on its texts, and in teaching its meaning are not listening to it themselves but only using it as a tool of their trade — reading the newspaper and ignoring the voice across the table? Scripture is sabotaged.

Three conditions contribute to the takeover of the heard word by the printed word. The first is a remarkable invention, the second is an unfortunate education, and the third is a faulty job description. Naming these conditions is the first step in recovering the primacy of the ear over the eye in attending to the word of God in Scripture.

$$\begin{matrix} \bullet & \bullet & \bullet \\ \bullet & \bullet & \bullet \end{matrix}$$

The remarkable invention is movable type. In 1437 Gutenberg invented movable type and in a short time books were being printed and put in the hands of people all over Europe. Until this time all books were laboriously handwritten. Books were, therefore, expensive and rare. Holy Scripture, an especially long book, was very expensive. Copies were chained to library tables to prevent theft. Since books were rare, readers were also rare, for what good did it do to read when there was not much around to read? When Scripture was read, it was ordinarily read aloud so that nonreaders, who were in the overwhelming majority, had access to the word. The written word was restored to a living voice in these settings. Reading was an oral act and a community event.

King Ahasuerus, when he couldn't sleep at night and wanted diversion, did not get a detective story and read himself to sleep; he was read to, *hearing* the words. When the Christians in St. John's seven Asian congregations came together to attend to the word of God written to them out of the Patmos vision, they did not read it with their eyes; they listened to it with their ears: "Blessed is he who reads aloud the words of the prophecy, and blessed are those who hear . . ." (Rev. 1:3). St. Anthony, the first Christian monk, happened to overhear Jesus' words to the rich young ruler read aloud and believed that he heard Jesus speaking directly to him.

In the pre-Gutenberg world people did not read, as we say, "to themselves." They *listened,* even when it was their own voice that was setting the sound waves in motion, to the re-voiced words of the author. One person reads aloud, other people listen in silence.

But Gutenberg's invention changed all that. A thorough-going orality in which the word held people in a listening community gave way to discrete individuals silently reading books alone. Mass-produced, inexpensively published books generated a motivation to read, which developed into a widespread literacy that changed the act of reading from an oral-aural community event into a silent-private visual exercise. Through the previous centuries when virtually every act of reading revoiced the written words, the connection with the living voice was emphatic. Today, when nearly all reading is silent, the connection with the living voice is remote.

That hundreds of millions of Bibles are published and distributed is often treated as an immense boon. And it is, but "this ease of access, when misused becomes a curse. When we read more books, look at more pictures, listen to more music, than we can possibly absorb the result of such gluttony is not a cultured mind but a consuming one; what it reads, looks at, listens to, is immediately forgotten, leaving no more traces behind it than yesterday's newspaper."[2] I do not wish the withdrawal of so much as a single Gospel of John from the general

---

2. W. H. Auden, *Secondary Worlds* (New York: Random House, 1968), p. 128.

distribution. All the same, Gutenberg's legacy is a mixed blessing and we must be prepared to deal with the consequences. Walter Ong has meditated long and interestingly on this phenomenon and is convinced that after six centuries of immersion in print we are

> the most abject prisoners of the literate culture in which we have matured. Even with the greatest effort, contemporary man finds it exceedingly difficult, and in many instances quite impossible, to sense what the spoken word actually is. He feels it as a modification of something which normally is or ought to be written.[3]

And the written and printed word of Scripture has become synonymous with the word of God. We assume that if we have it in print we have it, period. Bible equals word of God without discussion and without the faintest realization that to equate the bound book "Bible" with the "word of God" would not have been comprehensible to most of our Christian ancestors. There was no individualized "I" or "me" in relation to Scripture; it was always "we" or "us." There was no taking "a stand" on it as if it were a thing, for it was always the occasion of a sounding forth, a speaking out that the community sat *under* (lectern and pulpit are raised above the nave not only to facilitate hearing but also to signal the nature of the action: the congregation does not look *down on* or *at* a book curiously but sits *under* its word obediently).

Still, all is not lost. There are enclaves all over the world where the Bible continues to be read aloud and listened to by people who by inclination and habit much prefer to read it in the convenience and comfort of their private homes. For among

---

3. Walter Ong, S.J., *The Presence of the Word* (New Haven: Yale University Press, 1967), p. 19.

believers God is thought of always as "speaking" to human beings, not as writing to them. "The orality of the mindset in the biblical text is overwhelming"[4] and powerful enough, even centuries after Gutenberg, to maintain itself by voice at least at the liturgical services where people present themselves before God.

: : :

The unfortunate education has come about through the displacement of learning by schooling. Learning is a highly personal activity carried out in personal interchange: master and apprentice, teacher and student, parent and child. In such relationships the mind is trained, the imagination disciplined, ideas explored, concepts tested, behavioral skills matured in a context in which everything matters, in a hierarchy in which persons form the matrix. In true learning there is no division between mind and body. Learning facilitates the integration of inside and outside, the external world and the internal spirit. The classic methods of learning are all personal: dialogue, imitation, and disputation. The apprentice observes the master as the master learns; the master observes the apprentice as the apprentice learns. The learning develops through relationships expressed in gesture, intonation, posture, rhythm, emotions, affection, admiration. And all of this takes place in a sea of orality — voices and silences.

The archetype of learning is the infant and parent relationship, in which both, parent as much as infant, mature and develop competence in living as whole persons in a large world. This model for learning is so deeply embedded in the human

---

4. Walter Ong, S.J., *Orality and Literacy* (New York: Methuen, 1982), p. 75.

condition and has worked so well across the centuries that it seems unthinkable to abandon it in preference for the small segment of this complex process that can be reproduced in a laboratory. But it has been, and the laboratory is called a school. "School" is a blatant and ignorant misnaming — the Greek *scholē* means leisure. For the Greeks it was the protected space and time provided for the cultivation of unhurried personal relationships in conversation and games, with guidance but without interference. The contemporary school with its grades and periods and subjects is light-years removed from that.

Schooling is very different from learning. In schooling persons count for very little. Facts are memorized, information assimilated, examinations passed. Teachers are subjected to a supervision that attempts to insure uniform performance, which means that everyone operates as much alike as possible and is rewarded insofar as the transfer of data from book to brain is made with as little personal contamination as possible. In schooling, the personal is reduced to the minimum: standardized tests, regulated teachers, information-oriented students.

Since it is difficult to reduce children to abstractions all at once, learning maintains a precarious ascendancy over schooling for a few years. But inexorably the proportions shift until it is both possible and common for a student to graduate from a high school in which not a single teacher recognizes him or her by name, with the record of schooling summarized on a transcript in number, the most abstract of languages. Learning, a most intricately personal process, will not submit to such summarizing.

In our society there is no escaping such schooling. We are all products of it. The reading skills that we acquire under such conditions are inevitably attentive primarily to the informational: we are taught to read for the factual, the useful, the relevant. Most pastors have twenty years or so of such training. We read to pass examinations, to find out how to parse a Greek verb or to run a church office. If we read occasionally to divert ourselves on a cold winter's night it is not counted as serious reading. We are not systematically taught over these twenty years (I don't count an occasional course as "training") to pick up nuance and allusion, catching the meaning and intent of the living voice behind the words on the page. As a result we are impatient with metaphor and irritated at ambiguity. But these are the stock-in-trade of persons, the most unpredictable of creatures, using language at their most personal and best. Our schooling has narrowed our attitude toward reading: we want to know what is going on so that we can get on our way. If it is not useful to us in doing our job or getting a better one, we don't see the point.

By associating reading so thoroughly with schooling, we are habituated to looking for information when we read rather than being in relationship with a person who once spoke and then wrote so that we could listen to what was said. Language, of course, does provide information, and books are conveniently accessible containers for it. But the primary practice of language is not in giving out information but being in relationship. That primacy does not change when it is written. The primary reason for a book is to put a writer into relation with readers so that we can listen to his or her stories and find ourselves in them, listen to his or her songs and sing along with them, listen to his or her arguments and argue with them, listen to his or her answers and question them. The Scriptures are almost entirely this kind of book. If we read them impersonally with an information-gathering mind, we misread them.

The sheer proliferation of words via print devalues them and makes our task even more difficult. Schooling contributes to this devaluation by treating books as containers for information. Once they have been emptied of their contents (by getting the information out of them), they are discarded. (Maybe *that* is why so many Bibles are bought each year in America — on the principle of the paper bag that holds useful and holy information for baptism, confirmation, wedding, conversion, solace, anniversary, loneliness, bereavement, anxiety, or whatever. After you get your groceries home you discard the bag. When you need groceries again you get another bag. A market for paper bag Bibles would be endless — as it indeed seems to be.) The most common form of reading matter today is the newspaper, which is thrown away when it has been read. No pre-Gutenberg person would have done that. Every piece of writing was the record of a once-living voice and the means of bringing that voice to life again in the reader's ear. Written words were *symbols*. A symbol is not the same as the spoken word but the means for getting access to it. In ancient Greece a *symbolon* was a visible sign, a ticket, sometimes a broken coin or other object the matching parts of which were held separately by each of two contracting parties.[5] Every good book is such a symbol — writer and reader coming together joining the separate but matched parts, mouth and ear, and then, incredibly, the mouth speaking, the ear listening. Holy Scripture is a *symbolon,* a good book in just that way.

∴ ∴

The faulty job description has been written by customers in a consumer society. Historically, a unique thing has taken place in our society. The causes are multiple but the effect is single: everyone is a customer. We have been trained to think of ourselves and then to behave as consumers. We are known by

---

5. Ong, *The Presence of the Word,* p. 323.

what we buy. We measure the health of our nation and the success of our lives in terms of per capita income and gross national product. If people save what they earn instead of spend it, the nation gets sick. If we devote too much time to creating something enduring and beautiful without calculating its cost-efficiency, we damage the economy. If we look too long without buying, we retard progress. If we give away too much without counting the cost, we interfere with the market. If a politician running for office asks the question, "Are you better off now than you were four years ago?" everyone interprets that "better off" in terms of what money they have on hand to spend. I am worth what I spend.

No pastor is exempt from this conditioning. Our educators train us superbly in the acquisition of goods. Marshall McLuhan often remarked with dismay that the advertising budget of our nation exceeded by several times the school budget, and that the people who ran the advertising agencies were, with a few exceptions, far more able than those who ran the schools: "The classroom cannot compete with the glitter and the billion dollar success and prestige of this commercial education . . . disguised as entertainment and which by-passes the intelligence while operating on the will and the desires."[6]

If I receive my primary social identity as a consumer, it follows that my primary expectation of the people I meet is that I get something from them for which I am prepared to pay a price. I buy merchandise from the department store, health from the physician, legal power from the lawyer. Does it not follow that in this kind of society my parishioner will have commercialized expectations of me? None of the honored professions has escaped commercialization, so why should the

---

6. Marshall McLuhan, *The Mechanical Bride* (New York: Vanguard Press, 1951), p. 72.

pastorate? This has produced in our time the opprobrious practice of pastors manipulating their so-called flocks on the same principles that managers use to run supermarkets.

The question operates subliminally, shaping my behavior: what do people want from me, their pastor? Something surely along the order of a better life: encouragement, insight, consolation, formulas that enable them to get along better in a difficult world, that uplift them (a friend calls this "brassiere theology"). We, of course, are conditioned to comply. Why should we not please the people who pay our salaries if we can do it with good conscience? And why should not our consciences be good, ratified as they are by the vote of congregation after congregation? This consumerism shapes us without our knowing it. There is nothing in our lives that it does not touch in one way or another.

This acquisitive mode is so culturally expected and congregationally rewarding that it cannot fail to affect our approach to the Scriptures. When we sit down to read the Scriptures we already have an end product in view: we want to find something useful for people's lives, to meet their expectations of us as pastors who deliver the goods. If someone says to me, "I don't get anything out of reading Scripture," my knee-jerk response is, "I will show you how to read it so that you can get something out of it." The operative word is "get." I will help you be a better consumer. By this time the process is so far advanced that it is nearly irreversible. We have agreed, my parishioners and I, to treat the Bible as something useful for what they can use out of it. I, a pastor shaped by their expectations, help them to do it. At some point I cross over the line and am doing it myself — looking for an arresting text for a sermon, looking for the psychologically right reading in a hospital room, looking for evidence of the truth of the Trinity. The verb *looking* has taken over. I am no longer listening to a voice, not listening to

the God to whom I will give a response in obedience and faith,
becoming the person he is calling into existence. I am looking
for something that I can use to do a better job, for which people
will give me a raise if I do it conspicuously well enough.

: : :
: : :

These three powerful, hard-to-detect influences operate quietly
behind our backs and subvert the very nature of Scripture,
which is to provide a means for *listening* to the word of God.
Our immersion in these conditions is nearly total. Is it possible
to "get out of the whale"?

Yes, but not easy. Analysis is a lever for prying us loose
from our deaf and dumb cultural imprisonment. It is possible
to see that no mere *reading* of Scripture has integrity as a thing
in itself. It is but one element in a four-beat sequence: speaking,
writing, reading, listening. The genius of the book is that it
provides the means by which a speaker can be linked to a
listener without being in the same room or in the same century.
The two middle terms of the sequence are subordinate to the
first term (speaking) and the final term (listening); the book
(combining writer and reader) is in between, tissue that connects the speaker's mouth with the listener's ear, living organs
both. Writing and reading, which is to say *books,* are activities
in service of the speaking voice and listening ear. If they are
not kept in that service but become things in their own right,
they displace the primary reality with something less and other
— dead objects instead of living organs.

Reading, as we typically practice it, disconnects the terms
of the sequence by pulling out the two middle ones and valuing
them for their own sake. We hardly notice that violence has
been done since the elimination of the living voice at one end
and the listening ear at the other in favor of the written and

read book right before us serves the purpose of an impersonal, technological society so admirably. But a few people notice. Poets, parents, and spouses do, for essential aspects of their identity are called into question the moment words are no longer alive in speaking and listening. And pastors must notice, for we are involved in a way of life and a commitment to a reality that are emphatically personal and stubbornly relational. Our task is to get enough distance from our culture so that our theological conviction *that* God speaks has the time and space to hear the word he speaks and not just read about it.

Pastors must not only notice; they must counterattack. Given the circumstances, this is not easy. Gutenberg gave me an inexpensive book that I can own and carry with me wherever I go, encouraging the illusion that I have its contents in my pocket or purse, a possession over which I exercise control. My schooling gave me an authoritative text in which I can look up reliable information regarding the furniture of heaven and the temperature of hell. My consumerism gave me a best-selling manual that I can use to make life better on gloomy nights and to whip my congregation into a shape fit for eternity. I live, am educated, and make my living in a world that treats all books in this way and makes no exception for a book just because it is blessed with the adjective "holy." And so the speaking voice of God and the listening ear of the human — the very things that led to the writing, reading, copying, and translating of Scripture in the first place — are given a quiet and decent burial. Paul was right: "the letter kills" (2 Cor. 3:6, NIV).

$$\cdot \ \cdot \ \cdot$$
$$\cdot \ \cdot \ \cdot$$

Paul was also hopeful, believing as he did that "the Spirit gives life." It revives not only dead bodies and dead souls but also dead letters. So besides critically evaluating Gutenberg's invention, complaining about our schooling, and damning Adam Smith for turning us into such energetically diligent consumers, something must be done about it. But something *has* been done about it. When we locate exactly where it took place and how it works, we can get on with it.

A brilliantly conceived metaphor in Psalm 40:6 provides a pivot on which to turn the corner; literally it reads: "ears thou hast dug for me" (*'az'nayim karîtha lî*). It is puzzling that no translator renders the sentence into English just that way. They all prefer to paraphrase at this point, presenting the meaning adequately but losing the metaphor: "thou hast given me an open ear" (RSV). But to lose the metaphor in this instance is not to be countenanced; the Hebrew verb is "dug."

Imagine a human head with no ears. A blockhead. Eyes, nose, and mouth, but no ears. Where ears are usually found there is only a smooth, impenetrable surface, granitic bone. God speaks. No response. The metaphor occurs in the context of a bustling religious activity deaf to the voice of God: "sacrifice and offering thou dost not desire . . . burnt offering and sin offering" (40:6). How did these people know about these offerings and how to make them? They had *read* the prescriptions in Exodus and Leviticus and followed instructions. They had become religious. Their eyes read the words on the Torah page and rituals were formed. They had read the Scripture words accurately and gotten the ritual right. How did it happen that they had missed the message "not required"? There must be something more involved than following directions for unblemished animals, a stone altar, and a sacrificial fire. There is: God is speaking and must be listened to. But what good is a speaking God without listening human ears? So God gets a pick and shovel and digs through the cranial granite, opening a passage that will give access to the interior depths, into the mind and heart. Or — maybe we are not to imagine a smooth expanse of skull but something like wells that have been stopped up with refuse: culture noise, throw-away gossip, garbage chatter. Our ears are so clogged that we cannot hear God speak. God, like Isaac who dug again the wells that the Philistines had filled, redigs the ears trashed with audio junk.

The result is a restoration of Scripture: eyes turn into ears. The Hebrew sacrificial ritual included reading from a book, but the reading had degenerated into something done and watched. The business with the scroll was just part of the show, a verbal ingredient thrown into the ritual pot because the recipe called for it. Now with *ears* newly dug in the head of this person, a *voice* is heard calling, inviting. The hearer responds: "Lo, I come; in the roll of the book it is written of me; I delight to do thy will, O my God; thy law is within my heart" (40:7-8). The act of reading has become an act of listening. The book is discovered to have a voice in it directed to the reader-become-listener: "it is written of *me*." The words on the paper that were read with the eye are now heard with the ear and invade the heart: "I delight to do thy will . . . thy law is within my heart." God's word ("thy will"), which had been objectified in a written word ("thy law"), now is personalized in an answering and worshiping word ("my heart"). The act of reading becomes an act of listening. What was written down is revoiced: "I have told the glad news . . . I have not restrained my lips" (40:9). No longer is God's word merely written; it is voiced. The *ear* takes over from the *eye* and involves the *heart*.

Listening is back. The dynamic sequence has been restored. The psalm began with God listening: "I waited patiently for the Lord; he inclined to me and *heard* my cry" (40:1). Now the psalmist listens. God has dug through his thick skull and opened a passage for hearing. The living voice of God is attended by the human ear. The consequence, as always when God's word works, is gospel ("glad news of deliverance," "thy saving help"; 40:9, 10). It was a medieval commonplace that the organ of conception in the Virgin Mary was the ear.

Listening to Scripture, of course, presupposes reading Scripture. We have to read before we can listen. But we can read without going on to listen. Reading Scripture accurately and understandingly is one of the most difficult tasks under the sun. Gilbert Highet, the classicist, used to say that anyone who reads the Bible and isn't puzzled at least half the time doesn't have his mind on what he is doing. When we move from reading to listening, the already formidable difficulties are compounded by the serpentine difficulties of the self. Is it any wonder that so many ventures into listening slide back into the rut of reading?

Happily, we are not left to our own devices in these difficulties. The God who wills to reveal himself to us in word also wills our listening and provides for it. St. John tells us that the word of God that brings creation into being and salvation into action became flesh in Jesus, the Christ. Jesus is the word of God. One large dimension of St. John's Gospel shows Jesus bringing men and women into conversation with God — no longer merely reading the Scriptures, at which many of them were quite adept, but listening to *God,* which they hardly guessed was possible. This succession of conversation was closely followed and believingly entered into — Mary at Cana, Nicodemus at night, the Samaritan woman, the Bethzatha paralytic, the disputatious Pharisees, the Jerusalem blind man, the Bethany sisters, the Greek tour group, and then all of it gathered up into the profound crucifixion-eve conversation that took a marvelous turn at the end, the Son's conversation shifting from his disciples to his Father. At no place in St. John's Gospel is the word of God simply there — carved in stone, painted on a sign, printed in a book. The word is always *sound:* words spoken and heard, questioned and answered, rejected and obeyed, and, finally, prayed. Christians in the early church were immersed in these conversations and it changed the way they read the Scriptures: now it was all voice. They heard Jesus speaking off of every page of the Scriptures. When they preached and taught they did not expound texts; they preached "Jesus" — a living person with a living voice. They were not "reading in" Jesus to their Scriptures; they were *listening* as if for the first time and hearing that word that was in the beginning with God and through whom all things were made, and whom they had seen and touched, now hearing the word of God made alive for them in the resurrection. The dead body of Jesus was alive; so was the dead letter of Moses.

St. Matthew, St. Mark, and St. Luke employ a different method than St. John's but continue his emphasis as they shift our sensory reliance from the eye to the ear. These three present Jesus as a teacher whose characteristic form of teaching is the parable. The parable is an oblique way of coming at the truth, especially useful in getting past the defenses of those who are so familiar with it that they feel superior to it. Each of these synoptic writers makes his own selection of parables, suiting the different emphases that he is developing. They all agree, though, that the first parable is the parable of the sower and the four soils, a parable about hearing. This is the entrance parable, standing guard over everything else that Jesus will say. This parable denies us the option of reducing the word of God to a book; the primary target of the word is the ear. Jesus is speaking the seed words of God into our ears: pavement ears in which no seed can germinate, rocky ears in which no seed can sink roots, weedy ears in which no seed can mature, and good-soil ears in which all seed bears fruit. The greatest thing going on in this history, in this earth is that God is speaking. The dominical command is *Listen:* "He who has ears to hear, let him hear" (Mark 4:9 and parallels). The command reverberates for decades through the early church communities, reappears at the outset of the *Revelation,* "Blessed is he who reads and *those who hear,*" and then modulates into the seven famous repetitions of Jesus' imperative that pull every word-weary reader that ever stood in a pulpit or sat in a pew into an alive listening to the word that knows, rebukes, commends, encourages, promises, invites, and ends up, as it started out, making all things new (Rev. 2:7, 11, 17, 29; 3:6, 13, 22; and also 13:9).

Can any pastor in good conscience be content to leave the written words of Scripture on the page for the eye to read? Our business is with ears.

> O learn to read what silent love hath writ.
> To hear with eyes belongs to love's fine wit.[7]

---

7. William Shakespeare, Sonnet 23, in *Shakespeare's Sonnets,* ed. Douglas Bush and Alfred Harbage (Baltimore: Penguin Books, 1961), p. 45.

V

Contemplative Exegesis

I N Herman Melville's novel *White Jacket* one of the sailors takes sick with severe stomach pains. Dr. Cuticle, the ship's surgeon, is delighted to have a patient with something more challenging to his art than blisters. He diagnoses appendicitis. Several shipmates are impressed into nursing service. The deckhand is laid out on the operating table and prepared for surgery. Dr. Cuticle goes at his work with verve and skill. He makes his cuts with precision, and, on the way to excising the diseased organ, points out interesting anatomical details to the attendants around the table, who had never before seen the interior of an abdomen. He is absorbed in his work, and obviously good at it. All in all it is an impressive performance, but the sailor attendants are, to a man, not impressed but appalled. The poor patient, by the time he has been sewn up, has been a long time dead on the table. Dr. Cuticle, enthusiastic in his surgery, hadn't noticed. The sailors, shy in their subservience, didn't tell him.[1]

---

1. Herman Melville, *White Jacket* (Evanston, IL: Northwestern University Press, 1970).

Scriptural exegesis is surgical work: cutting through layers of history, culture, and grammar; laying bare the skeletal syntax and grammatical muscle; excising mistakes that were introduced inadvertently in the transmission of the text; repairing misunderstandings that have crept into interpretations across the centuries; observing the incredible and fascinating complexity of the organism as the hidden parts are exposed to view.

This work is essential to the church's comprehension of the Scriptures. Pastors are trained for it. In regard to exegetical technology, we are far better furnished than earlier generations. Today's surgeon, impressively equipped with electronic, nuclear, and chemical technologies, is no more advanced over his predecessors than we are over ours. We know more Hebrew than Jerome, practice a better historical method than Augustine, and understand comparative grammar better than Calvin. The twentieth-century pastor in a rural Nebraska parish has more and better exegetical tools at his fingertips than entire faculties could muster as recently as one hundred years ago. Manuscript discoveries, archaeological excavations, and philological studies have piled mountains of new material on the desks and into the libraries of the church's scholars. The best minds in the world are among those who examine and evaluate these findings and then render historical, theological, and textual understandings of Scripture that are simply beyond praise. It is hard to believe, but on most pages of Scripture we can arrive at a more accurate reading of the text than anyone since its first generation of readers. There is much that we do not yet know, some that we will never know, but what our Scripture scholars and theological libraries provide us is staggeringly impressive. And not a pastor in the land is denied access to this exegetical wealth — on the contrary, he or she is invited, sometimes ordered, to become competent in it. Access to theological education is unrestricted, the professors learned, the libraries well-stocked, the time allotted for study adequate.

All the same, things are not at all well. In parish after parish, pastors work away on Scripture with skilled diligence. Parishioners stand around, working up the nerve to say something. It seems a shame to interrupt: the pastor is so good at it, knows so much, so much enjoys explaining the origin of this story, the significance of this custom, the root meaning of this verb. But the fact is that the patient is dead. No matter that the pastor brings superb exegetical technique to the text; there is no corresponding comprehension that the church's concern with Scripture is with *God* — a living, speaking God. Pastor after pastor works away with all the technical skill and personal insensitivity of Dr. Cuticle. Despite the unsurpassed academic training that American pastors receive, it looks very much as if no generation of pastors that we know about historically has been so embarrassingly ill-trained in the contemplation of Scripture.

No amount of technical exegetical skill compensates for a failure to attend to the "patient" — Scripture as the living word of God. The pastor's exegetical task is in service to the aliveness of this word. Exegesis, if it is to serve the church's life and be congruent with the pastor's calling, must be *contemplative* exegesis.

Contemplative exegesis is not a new thing. It is the kind of exegesis that has been practiced through most of the church's life. Which means that the remedy for our exegetical embarrassment is not innovation but recovery. The recovery of contemplative exegesis does not mean jettisoning so much as a single item of current exegetical fact or insight. Entrusted as we are with proclaiming and teaching the text of Scripture, we are required to know as much about it as we are able from every quarter: grammatical, theological, historical. The exegetically careless pastor should be sued, if there were a way to do it, with the same diligence and on the same grounds as the surgeon who uses a septic scalpel. Contemplative exegesis does not bypass or denigrate technical exegesis; it is diligent about it. All the same, as Melville was telling our country more than a hundred years ago, *technique* is not healing; *information* is not knowledge. There is something *alive* in a body, in a book. Any pastor who forgets or ignores that enters the pulpits and lecterns across the land as the comic pastiche of Dr. Cuticle.

The recovery of contemplative exegesis begins with a realization that a word, any word, is originally and basically a phenomenon of sound, not print. Words are spoken before they are written. Words are heard before they are read. Most words in the Scriptures had a long oral existence before they were written. These words were preached and taught, sung and prayed in worshiping communities for years, decades, sometimes centuries, before being written. They were passed from mouth to ear. These words were not shelved in libraries but resonated from ear to ear through the generations. The only words that Jesus, the word made flesh, wrote were in sand and were dissolved in the next rain. But those were the only words of his that were lost to us, or at least the only ones of significance. Everything that he spoke that is necessary for our salvation was heard and savored, pondered and preached, ruminated and taught, remembered and repeated in the dynamic interplay of bold lips and eager ears in the believing communities.

This thoroughgoing *orality* of the biblical communities is the immense, subterranean reality flowing underneath the biblical writings, and it leads to reflection on what the word, as word, is. That God reveals himself by word has enormous import for the pastor who is at work at exegesis.

A speaking voice originates in an interior and is directed to another interior. Sight deals with surfaces; sound deals with interiors. Sound is an inwardness that becomes an "utterance," an "outerance" that, when listened to, becomes inward in another. My voice really goes out of me, but it calls not to something outside but to the inwardness of another. Walter Ong, who has reflected on these matters more thoroughly than anyone I know, says a word "is the call of one interior through an exterior to another interior."[2]

Much more than in the world of sight, sound involves us in the personally alive. We *tell* our inmost thoughts and feelings, we do not *show* them. We do not cut a person open to find what is inside, but listen to an utterance that then enters, gets inside us. It is by exchanging sounds, not snapshots, with each other that revelation takes place and relationship becomes intimate.

Ong, who contends for the unique appropriateness of word rather than picture as the means by which God reveals his inwardness to our inwardness, develops a perspective on exegetical practice that pastors must master:

> The word as sound signals interiority and mystery (a certain inaccessibility even in intimacy) . . . , two aspects of existence which we need to keep alive today. It also signals holiness — the holiness of the individual person and, in Hebrew and Christian teaching, the holiness of God. For holiness is inaccessibility, a sense of distance to be maintained, a sense of what is taboo: the Hebrew *kadosh*, generally translated as holy, at root means separated. The spoken word is somehow always radically inac-

---

2. Walter Ong, *The Presence of the Word* (New Haven: Yale University Press, 1967), p. 309.

cessible; it flees us, eludes our grasp, escapes when we try to immobilize it. Coming from the deep interior, it comes from a region to which we have no direct entry, the personal consciousness of another, the consciousness from what it means in the mouth of anyone else.[3]

This phenomenological fact, that all words originate as sounds, means that all words are events. And not journalistic events that can be reported, but revelatory events that enter and involve us. No word, even after it is written, is inert. This is a theological fact regarding Scripture, but it is also a biological/physical fact regarding all words, in and out of Scripture: something *seen* may be inert; something *heard,* never. When we hear a sound — a voice whispering, thunder clapping, a tree falling, a dog growling, an infant crying — something is happening and so we had better be alert.

It follows that the widespread academic practice, which pastors have unhappily fallen in with, of treating the Scriptures primarily if not exclusively as a phenomenon of print, a textbook written to provide us with information about God or doctrine or morals or religious history, is a fatal error. A textbook is the one thing that the Scriptures most emphatically are not. And the worshiping church at worship has never so much as entertained such a notion. Something much larger and more active is perceived: a verbal *matrix* in which the believing behavior of a worshiping community is shaped and renewed. God both was and is active in Scripture. Not everybody, of course, believes that, but the *church's* scholars and theologians (I have little regard for the opinion of the university in these matters) believe that. Scripture is revelation. When a living God reveals himself the result is a living truth.

───────────

3. Ibid., p. 315.

The moment, though, that the truth is written we find ourselves up to our knees in a paradox: ink on paper is not living. How can a living word be conveyed by means of a dead word? Pastors do their work in the midst of this paradox: dead letters written by human hands are living words spoken by God. But that is not the way we commonly treat words in books. Books are *things* that we *see,* not listen to. We buy them and sell them. We open them and close them. We lend them and borrow them. And because Scripture, whatever else it is, comes into our sensory experience primarily as a book, it is possible (probable, in fact, given the large quantity of books that we observe and handle) that we misconstrue this living revelation as inanimate information. The church's task (and its pastors have a large measure of responsibility in carrying out this task) is to prevent this misconstruction — to prevent *revelation,* which always involves personal histories and personal responses, from being treated as *information,* which usually involves impersonal facts and abstract ideas.

My pastoral concern, it should be clear, is not to argue a particular theological position on the inspiration of Scripture, but simply to represent the unbroken consensus of Israel and church in regard to Scripture: that a living God speaks a living word and that the Holy Scriptures are the written representation of that word. We read Scripture in order to listen again to the word of God *spoken,* and when we do, we hear him *speak.* Somehow or other these words *live.*[4]

Appreciation for the fact that these words are *written* — this marvelous book, these incredible sentences — can hardly

---

4. Of the theologians who have dealt with the "somehow or other," I have most benefited from the works of Karl Barth, *Church Dogmatics,* I/1, 2 (Edinburgh: T. & T. Clark, 1936, 1956), and Hans Urs von Balthasar, *The Glory of God* (San Francisco: Ignatius Press, 1982), 1:527-677.

be overdone. That the word was written is a gift quite beyond compare. But if the appreciation is not discerning it blurs into superstition (treating the Bible as a totem) or hardens into arrogance (using the Bible as a club to pound the truth into others). Words work differently when they are read than when they are heard: a discerning appreciation keeps the pressure on all who read Scripture continually to return it to its originating context in worship and *hear* the word of God.

The contrast between Greek culture and Hebrew/Christian culture is instructive at this point. The ancient Hebrews and ancient Greeks differed in their primary sensory orientation: the Hebrews tended to think of understanding as a kind of hearing, whereas the Greeks thought of it as a kind of seeing.[5] Northrop Frye has pointed out that Greek culture revolved around two powerful visual events: the nude in sculpture and the drama in literature.[6] In the theater words are spoken, but the theater itself is primarily a visual experience, as the origin of the word (*theasthai,* to see) indicates. A religion with a lot of gods and goddesses requires statues or pictures to distinguish them from each other. In Greek culture the divine was looked at and talked about. The Olympian pantheon provided plots for the drama, patrons for the games, and images for the temples. The gods were external to the life of the people. The activities and speech of the gods were conceived visually, a spectacle to which the people were spectators.

The Hebrew/Christian culture, on the other hand, revolved around two audio events: the unseen God speaking his word to Moses and the people at Sinai, and the word becoming flesh in Jesus, the Christ. The Hebrews, followed by the Chris-

---

5. Ong, *The Presence of the Word,* p. 3.

6. Northrop Frye, *The Great Code* (New York: Harcourt Brace Jovanovich, 1982), pp. 117-18.

tians, forbade images and produced no plays. They listened to the one God. His word made them who they were and called them into pilgrimage and discipleship. When they met together they did not look at a statue or watch a play; they heard a command and answered with a prayer. The difference is radical and revolutionizing.

Hebrews and Christians, aware of the enormous difference between themselves and the Greeks, and the critical necessity of preserving their *word*-ness over against the Greek *image*-ness, kept their distance from nude bodies and theaters. From our perspective that looks like prudery, and maybe it did decline into that, but at root it was protection against the danger of the powerful visual stimuli of statuary and drama seducing them into a religion of aestheticism, away from the moral/spiritual intensities of faith. They knew how easy it was for the ardor of obedient listening to be diluted into amused watching, and they took measures to guard their aural concentration. They sensed that surrounding themselves with all those god-images reduced them to less than they knew themselves to be. Religion as entertainment is always more attractive, but it is also less true. It is pretty poor stuff compared to the word. Paul sarcastically asked the Galatians if they preferred "the weak and beggarly elemental spirits, whose slaves you want to be once more?" (Gal. 4:9).

In Hellenistic Palestine, Herod the Great, a passionate builder, constructed seven huge amphitheaters across the country. He had a great love of all things Greek and wanted to proselytize his subjects to Greek ways. The amphitheaters were adorned with magnificent Greek and Roman statuary and seated large assemblies of people. His strategy was to immerse the population, through performances in these theaters, in Hellenism and bring his kingdom of people up to par with the best of the world's culture. These amphitheaters were the dominant architectural features in seven cities: Caesarea, Damascus, Gadara, Kanatha, Scythopolis, Philadelphia (modern Amman), and Jerusalem. All but the Jerusalem structure are still visible, impressive even in partial ruin.[7] No other first-century buildings rival them in size or beauty. The synagogues are chicken coops in comparison. The Temple in Jerusalem, rebuilt by Herod, was as lavish, but it was built not out of belief but for propaganda — Herod was courting favor with the Jews in order to make good Greeks out of them.

Given the number and strategically placed prominence of these Greek amphitheaters, it seems incredible that there is not a single mention of any of them in our New Testament. That is as unlikely an omission as if a detailed account of a great historical event in Washington, D.C., had no reference to any great building or monument in that city of beautiful buildings. But the omission throws into sharp relief what was central in the lives of those who wrote our Scriptures: the Christian community came into being *listening*, not *looking*. Their Lord had come among them preaching, teaching, and healing. He came without entourage. He did most of his work in obscurity. When they wrote the account of the spoken and heard, sung and prayed good news, it was as if those great theaters and the crowds that filled them week after week had never existed. And in a way they had not: there was no substance to them. They had all been exterior, a show. Meanwhile, the writers had been listening to a word that had penetrated their interiors and conceived new life in them. They wrote what they experienced — the word that healed and blessed, saved and judged. Noth-

---

7. We have it from Josephus that Herod built an amphitheater in Jerusalem. C. Schick discovered one south of the city in 1887, but it is not certain that it is Herodian. See the *Interpreters Dictionary of the Bible* (New York: Abingdon Press, 1962), 4:615.

ing that they had experienced could be carved into a statue or performed on a stage: *they* were the images of God, *they* were the tragic/comic plot of salvation. The consequence was Scripture; not statues or theaters where people gathered to look, but words before which people assembled to listen to sounds that shape great energies and purposes in us, our beginnings and our ends (*archē* and *telos*).

: :
:
: :

Contemplative exegesis means listening to the word as *sound,* the word that reveals out of one's interior; it also means receiving the words in the *form* in which they are given. For the *way* in which words are spoken is as important as what the words say. To alter the form is to alter the message, and sometimes to violate it. Biblical words come to us in the biblical story: contemplative exegesis is careful to listen to the story.

All words turn, eventually, into stories. Narrative is the most basic form of speech. If the recovery of contemplative exegesis begins with a realization that words are basically sounds that reveal, it matures with the recognition that when words are put together they form stories that shape. Whenever we open our mouths to speak, it isn't long before we are telling a story. Whenever we open our ears to listen, it isn't long before we are hearing a story. The most common and natural way to assemble words together is in story form. Words do not occur in isolation; they connect. And when they connect they make a narrative.

Words are also used in nonnarrative ways: to command, identify, direct, gossip, curse, explain, teach. But in these specialized utterances there is always an implicit narrative context that provides the conditions for comprehension.

Children are the perpetual evidence and reminder of this.

As soon as they acquire a working knowledge of the language, they demand stories. The people who tell the stories are their elders. We start out in language listening to stories; we end up, if we are fortunate, telling stories. In between, in the rush to make a living, check out the stock market quotations, learn to program a computer, put together a sermon, we often abandon story-listening and storytelling for what we suppose are more practical uses of language. But even then we are usually ready to listen to a story, or tell one, if we or someone important to us is in it.

This deep love of stories and widespread telling of them is cross-cultural. Everybody seems to do it. Illiterate primitives tell stories; highly educated scientists read stories; everyone in between can be found at some point or other during the day listening to, telling, or reading a story.

The universal demand for and appreciation of stories is rooted in the nature of the beings who use language and the nature of the language that we use. At some deep level we sense that the story is the only way adequately to account for ourselves and our world, and also the only way in which words can be used that comes close to doing justice to them. If words are, in fact, personally revelational and not merely signals to communicate data (the purpose and practice of words being to sound out of one interior into another), then what they sound out is story. Words do not add up to a list of definitions in a lexicon. Words do not amalgamate into an encyclopedia of information. Words do not congeal into free-floating oracles. Words become stories, each word connecting with the other, and in the interconnections showing forth meanings that have continuities, depicting characters and circumstances in ways that cohere with each other, developing in time and space among people.

Just as cells multiply and become a human body, so the multiplication of words becomes a story. That doesn't mean that all words are a story any more than that all cells are a body. It is useful from time to time, for purposes of healing, to examine a few cells in a cross section of bodily tissue under a microscope. But people who have bodies, insofar as they are wise, attend to them in their wholeness, live in them completely. There are also times when it is useful, for purposes of understanding, to subject words to etymological dissection and sentences to syntactical analysis. But it is words in their organic connectedness, story, that we are dealing with when we let the language operate fully.

None of us lives long enough or knows enough to listen to all the stories that language forms and hear them as one story. But just as each human body is representative of every other human body, so it is also with stories. Some bodies and some stories are more sound by nature and better developed by discipline than others, and so invite closer attention. For people of faith, the Bible is the story that is sound and developed. Here the language that God uses to reveal himself comes into story form that is most complete. When we listen to the word of God in Scripture, listening for what God is revealing out of himself, a story is shaped in our hearing; and the fact that it is *story* and not something else — systematic theology, moral instruction, wise sayings — has powerful implications for exegetical work. For just as words have a revealing quality to them, so stories have a shaping quality to them.

Why is the story so often dismissed as not quite adult? Why, among earnest pastors, is the story looked down upon as not quite serious? It is ignorance, mostly. The story is the most adult form of language, the most serious form into which language can be put. Among pastors, who have particular responsibilities for keeping the words of Scripture active in the mind and memory of the faith communities, an appreciation for the story in which Scripture comes to us is imperative.

Just as there is a basic human body (head, torso, two arms, two legs, etc.), so there is a basic story. All stories are different in detail (like all bodies) but the basic elements of story are always there. For the purposes of sharpening our recognition of and appreciation and respect for the essential narrative shape of Scripture, we need to distinguish only five elements.

First, there is a beginning and ending. All stories take place in time and are bounded by a past and a future. This large encompassing framework presumes both an original and a final goodness. We have an origin, way back somewhere, somehow, that is good (creation, Eden, Atlantis); we have a destination, someplace, sometime, that is good (promised land, heaven, utopia).

Second, a catastrophe has occurred. We are no longer in continuity with our good beginning. We have been separated from it by a disaster. We are also, of course, separated from our good end. We are, in other words, in the middle of a mess.

Third, salvation is plotted. Some faint memory reminds us that we were made for something better than this. Some faint hope lingers that we can do something about it. In the tension between the good origin and destiny and the present evil, a plan develops to get us out of the trouble we are in, to live better than we find ourselves, to arrive at our destination. This plan develops with two kinds of action, the battle and the journey: we must fight the forces that oppose our becoming whole; we must find our way through difficult and unfamiliar territory to our true home. The battle and journey motifs are usually intertwined. These battles and journeys are both interior (within the self) and exterior.

Fourth, characters develop. What people do is significant. Persons have names and dignity. They make decisions. Persons are not lead soldiers lined up and moved about arbitrarily; personalities develop in the course of the conflict and in the

120

passage of the journey, character and circumstance in dynamic interplay with each other. Some persons become better; some become worse. Nobody stays the same.

Fifth, everything has significance. Since "story" implies "author," nothing is in it by accident. Nothing is mere "filler." Chekov once said that if a writer puts a gun on the table in the first chapter, somebody has to pull the trigger by the last chapter. Every word connects with every other word in the author's mind, and so every detail, regardless of how it strikes us at first, belongs — and can be seen to belong if only we look long enough at it.

All the world's stories have these characteristics. The five elements can be more or less implicit or explicit, but they are there. With variations in emphasis and proportion, with shifts of perspective and invention of detail, they develop into trage-dies, comedies, epics, confessions, murder mysteries, and gothic romances. Poets, dramatists, novelists, children, and parents have developed millions of variations on these ele-ments; some of them have been written down.

What was written down in the Bible is a huge, sprawling account that contains subject matter from several cultures, lan-guages, and centuries. There are many things and people in it, written about in many different ways; but with all the seeming heterogeneity, it comes out as a story. Northrop Frye, coming at Scripture as a literary critic and not as a believer or theologian, in his careful study of it is convinced that this is its most important feature: "The emphasis on narrative, and the fact that the entire Bible is enclosed in a narrative framework, distin-guishes the Bible from a good many other sacred books."[8]

The Bible's basic story line is laid down in the Torah, the first five books. Creation is the good beginning, worked into

---

8. Frye, *The Great Code*, p. 198.

our memories with the rhythmic repetitions, "and God saw that it was good." The promised land is the good ending as Moses leads the people up to the border of Canaan and then leaves them with his Deuteronomy sermon ringing in their ears. In between is the catastrophe of the fall, succeeded by the plot of salvation worked out in pilgrimage — from Eden to Babel to Ur to Palestine to Egypt to wilderness to Jordan — and in fights with family, Egyptians, Amalekites, and Canaanites. Character development is shown in Abraham, Isaac, Jacob, Joseph, and Moses in major ways, and in numerous others on a smaller scale. The significance of every detail of existence is emphasized by including genealogical tables, ceremonial regulations, social observations, and rules for diet.

This story is repeated in the Gospels. The virgin birth is the good beginning, the ascension the good end. Catastrophe erupts in the Herodian massacre and threatens in the wilderness temptations. The salvation plot is worked out on a journey from Galilee to Jerusalem and in conflict with devils, disease, Pharisees, and disciples. The person of Jesus is prominent in the story, with Peter, James, and John in strong supporting roles. Much care is given to the details of geography, chronology, and conversation: nothing escapes signification — not a sparrow, not a hair of our heads.

The same story is told with a tighter focus in Holy Week. The hosanna welcome launches the good beginning, the resurrection marks the good ending. Judas's betrayal is the catastrophe. Salvation is plotted through the conflicts of trial, scourging, and crucifixion and on the journey from Bethany to upper room to Gethsemane to trial sites to Golgotha to the garden tomb. Jesus' words and actions exhibit the working out of the life of redemption, everything that he says and does being presented as revelatory. No detail is without significance: Mary's perfume, the centurian's comment.

The narrative that is explicit in Torah and Gospels is extended over the entire Scriptures by means of the canonical arrangement of the diverse books. The Hebrew canon is formed in three parts. The Torah (Genesis through Deuteronomy) sets down the basic story. The Prophets (Joshua through Malachi) take the basic story and introduce it into new situations across the centuries, insisting that it be believed and obeyed in the present, not merely recited out of the past. This involved a good deal of disruption and controversy. The Writings (Psalms through Chronicles) provide a reflective response to the story, assimilating and then responding to it in wisdom (Job and Proverbs) and in worship (Psalms).[9]

The New Testament has a parallel shape. The Gospels tell the basic story in a new Torah. The Epistles correspond to the Prophets as the story is told in an expanding world, preached and taught through continuing journeys and conflicts across multiple geographical and cultural settings around the Mediterranean basin. (Acts plays a double role here, part Torah, part Prophets; Luke, by writing a two-volume work, nicely expands the four Gospels into a five-volume Torah at the same time that he introduces the prophetical/apostolic lives of Peter and Paul.) James and the Revelation are equivalent to the Writings, summing up in wisdom (James) and worship (Revelation) the response of a people whose lives are shaped by the story that they have heard and told in faith.

What must be insisted upon in exegesis is that the Scriptures come to us in this precise, canonical shape, a deeply comprehensive narrative framework gathering all the parts — proverbs, commandments, letters, visions, case law, songs,

---

9. Walter Brueggemann shows the profound and extensive educational uses to which this canonical arrangement can be put in our communities of faith in *The Creative Word* (Philadelphia: Fortress Press, 1982).

prayer, genealogies — into the story, a unified structure of narrative and imagery.[10]

It is fatal to exegesis when this narrative sense is lost, or goes into eclipse. Every word of Scripture fits into its large narrative context in one way or another, so much so that the immediate context of a sentence is as likely to be eighty-five pages off in words written three hundred years later as to be the previous or the next paragraph. When the narrative sense is honored and nurtured, everything connects and meanings expand, not arbitrarily but organically — narratively. We see this at work in the narrative-soaked exegesis of a preacher like John Donne whose texts always lead us "like a guide with a candle, into the vast labyrinth of Scripture, which to Donne was an infinitely bigger structure than the cathedral he was preaching in."[11]

At the moment words are written down they immediately become what has been called "context free." The tone of voice, the smell in the air, the wind on the cheek — these are gone. Yet, when we carefully observe the way language actually works in our practice of it, we know that this living context in which we speak and hear words is critically important. Setting, tone, inflection, gesture, weather — all of this matters. Most of this context is lost in the act of writing. But one thing is not lost: the basic narrative form itself, language shaped into story.

Since this is the one part of the context that we do have, we must not let any part of it slip from our attention: the Genesis to Revelation context, the basic story laid down in

---

10. The literature on this is extensive. The symposium on story in *Theology Today* 32 (1975) provides a good orientation. Hans Frei gives us the best account of how the narrative of Scripture was lost to the present-day exegetical world. See his *The Eclipse of Biblical Narrative* (New Haven: Yale University Press, 1976).

11. Frye, *The Great Code*, p. 209.

Torah and Gospels, the intrusion of story into history by means of Prophets and Epistles, the gathering response and anticipation of closure in Psalms and Revelation.

Most misunderstandings come not from missed definitions but from missed contexts. Why do we miss another's meaning so frequently — in marriage, in international relations, in courtrooms? It is not because we do not understand the language; it is because we do not know the context. Professional listeners (counselors and therapists) spend hours listening to a person's story before they even begin to understand. They get the message in the first twenty minutes — why then does it take so long? What are they listening for? In a word, context: all the contexts of family and work, school and sex, feelings and dreams that intersect in the human. A word used in one context reverses meaning in another. Understanding another person intimately takes years; a lifetime is not enough. The more context we are familiar with, the more understanding we develop.

Whether in reading Scripture or in conversing around the kitchen table, an isolated sentence can only be misunderstood. The more sentences we have, the deeper the sense of narrative is embedded in our minds and imaginations and the more understanding is available. Matthew is incomprehensible separated from Exodus and Isaiah. Romans is an enigma without Genesis and Deuteronomy. Revelation is a crossword puzzle without Ezekiel and the Psalms.

∴ ∴

Words are sounds that reveal. Words make stories that shape. Contemplative exegesis means opening our interiors to these revealing sounds and submitting our lives to the story these words tell in order to be shaped by them. This involves a poet's respect for words and a lover's responsiveness to words.

125

Contemplative exegesis, then, involves these two matters: an openness to words that reveal and a submission to words that shape. Words are double dimensioned: they carry meaning from their source, and they carry influence to their destination. All words do this in one way or another. God's decision to use words as a means for revealing himself and shaping us means that we must pay attention both to what he says and to how he says it. Contemplative exegesis is not esoteric; it is not fancy. It simply means treating the tool with respect, not using an ax to hoe the garden.

VI

Gaza Notes

ON THE ROAD to Gaza I find the focus for my hermeneutical work as pastor: the Ethiopian reading Scripture and not understanding it; Philip guiding him into comprehension. The two men have nothing, it would seem, in common: not country, not race, not sexuality. The African has just been worshiping in Jerusalem, from which Philip has only recently been kicked out. The eunuch is on his way home to the court of Queen Candace of Ethiopia where he is minister of finance; the evangelist is on his way to Caesarea where he lives with his four daughters. They seem singularly ill-matched for a conversation that deals with fine discriminations and involves personal trust. Yet they undertake this joint venture in understanding a delicately nuanced and obscurely phrased passage in a five-hundred-year-old book. And it works. What unlikely meetings and surprising comprehensions take place across these pages of Scripture. And how important it is to be there: running to catch up, sitting to listen, willing to get wet.

Hermeneutics begins with a question: "Do you understand what you are reading?" (Acts 8:30). The play on words in Philip's Greek is untranslatable: *ginōskeis ha anaginōskeis?* The

difference between reading and understanding seems so slight
— a mere prefix (*ana*) in a Greek verb — that we are slow to
realize the abyss that separates what Isaiah wrote from what
we understand. Lessing called the gap between the written and
the read the "dirty ditch." The much that we know — lexical
definitions of the words, quality of the parchment, theology of
Deutero-Isaiah — is a lid over the bottomless pit of our ignorance. We ride along in uncomprehending familiarity with
the biblical text for years, in devout travel to and from Jerusalem, and then a well-timed question stops the chariot.

The question is answered with a question: "How can I,
unless someone guides me?" (v. 31). The questioner is questioned: Will you guide me? The word choice is critical: not
explain but *guide*. The Greek words for "explain" and "guide"
share the same verbal root, "to lead," and have a common
orientation in and concern for the text. But the explainer, the
exegete, leads the meaning out of the text; the guide, the *hodegete*,
leads *you* in the way (*hodos*) of the text. Pastoral-biblical hermeneutics presupposes exegesis but involves more. The African
invites Philip into the chariot to accompany him as his guide.
This is going to take some time. Philip has to make a choice: will
he stand alongside the chariot, providing information and answering questions about Scripture, exegetical work that comes
easily for him, or will he involve himself in a spiritual quest with
this stranger? Will I? It is the difference between the shopkeeper
who sells maps of the wilderness and the person who goes with
you into it, risking the dangers, helping to cook the meals, and
sharing the weather. Philip decides on *hodegesis*. He climbs into
the chariot and shares the journey.

Third question: "About whom, pray, does the prophet say
this, about himself or about someone else?" (v. 34). Philip's
answer was "Someone else," whereupon he guided him to Jesus.
Martin Luther insisted that we always read the Scriptures with

an eye for *was Christum triebet,* "what impels to Christ." This has nothing to do with an ignorant disregard for the plain meaning of the text or an arbitrary contempt for the writer's history and culture. The silly practice of pawing through Scripture, making referential connections between, say, "lamb" and "Jesus," has nothing in common with this. Rather, it is a conviction, born out of much reading of Scripture and much experience with Christ, that all the words of Scripture are contextually coherent in the word made flesh, Jesus. "Much reading of Scripture and much experience with Christ": that was Philip's hermeneutical course work. Philip and his deacon and apostle friends were not rummaging through Scripture trying to find something to justify their persecuted lives; they were simply awake to the obvious: if Scripture is God's word and if Jesus is God's word, then the two word forms are congruent with each other: the Scriptures are God's word in Jesus; Jesus is God's word in Scripture. They tested it out in their believing and worshiping lives. It worked. They had their hermeneutical principle.

"What is to prevent my being baptized?" (v. 36). Questions beget questions, each one cutting deeper than the last. This fourth question cuts deepest of all and reaches the inmost human, the heart-womb where eternal life is conceived and shaped. Hermeneutics is not a tidy, administrative process, going from point to point with syllogistic clarity. It meanders. It detours. It waits, sometimes in puzzlement, sometimes in wonder. But always it has a target. These Scriptures are not provided to feed our gossipy curiosity or legislate our barnyard morals: they examine our lives and invite our faith. God's word via Isaiah's scroll with the help of Philip's guidance searches its way through the labyrinthine muddle in the eunuch to his heart and evokes the basic question: "What is to prevent my being baptized?" All questions are, in one form or another, elements of quest that when patiently pursued arrive at baptism. The final question is not a query for more information but a request for a new life. The ink on the Isaiah scroll and the water in the Gaza creek are the sibling material forms by which a comprehending and obedient faith is assisted to birth. Gaza hermeneutics intends (or presumes) baptism and sends us on our way rejoicing.

Reading Scripture is not, it would seem, an autonomous activity. The solitary reader of Isaiah in the chariot on the Gaza road is interrupted by the Spirit-commanded Philip. The Spirit brings people together over Scripture — listening, questioning, conversing toward faith. The questioning reader was joined by the listening interpreter. Isaiah, dead but word-present in the scroll, made a third. The unseen but Spirit-present Christ became the fourth. It happened again, as it keeps on happening: "Where two or three are gathered together in my name, there I am in the midst of them."

I spend so much of my life along this particular stretch of the Gaza road. Sometimes I am running alongside the chariot, asking one question: sometimes, riding in the chariot, I am asking another — interpreting and interpreted by the Isaiah scroll.

> Always when I have to translate or to interpret a biblical text, I do so with fear and trembling, in an inescapable tension between the word of God and the words of man.
>
> MARTIN BUBER[1]

> I have known dozens of people who use the Bible as if it were a Rorshach test rather than a religious text. They read more into the ink than they read out of it.
>
> ELLEN GOODMAN[2]

---

1. Martin Buber, *Meetings*, ed. Maurice Freedman (La Salle, IL: Open Court, 1973), p. 54.
2. Ellen Goodman, *The Baltimore Sun*, June 15, 1979.

The Lord of the language is also the Lord of our listening to it.

KARL BARTH[3]

Holy Scripture is the garment which our Lord Christ has put on and in which He lets Himself be seen and found. This garment is woven throughout and so wrought together into one that it cannot be cut or parted.

MARTIN LUTHER[4]

In the vector which makes up the possibility of exegesis, method may be one component; but experience with the texts involved is another, and probably a more necessary and central one.

JAMES BARR[5]

Language is not speech, it is a full circle from word to sound to perception to understanding to feeling, to memorizing, to acting and back to the word about the act thus achieved. And before the listener can become a listener, something has to happen to him: he must expect.

EUGEN ROSENSTOCK-HUESSY[6]

Reading Scripture constitutes an act of crisis. Day after day, week after week, it brings us into a world that is totally at odds with the species of world that newspaper and television serve up to us on a platter as our daily ration of data for conversation and concern. It is a world where God is active

---

3. Karl Barth, *Church Dogmatics* I/1 (Edinburgh: T. & T. Clark, 1936), p. 208.

4. Quoted by Barth, *CD* I/2 (Edinburgh: T. & T. Clark, 1956), p. 484.

5. James Barr, *Old and New in Interpretation* (London: SCM Press, 1966), p. 199.

6. Eugen Rosenstock-Huessy, *Speech and Reality* (Norwich, VT: Argos Books, 1970), p. 145.

everywhere and always, where God is fiery first cause and not occasional afterthought, where God cannot be procrastinated, where everything is relative to God and God is not relative to anything. Reading Scripture involves a dizzying reorientation of our culture-conditioned and job-oriented assumptions and procedures. "The Scripture stories do not, like Homer's, court our favor, they do not flatter us that they may please us and enchant us — they seek to subject us, and if we refuse to be subjected we are rebels."[7] Scripture calls into question the domesticated accommodations we are busily arranging for the gospel. The crisis into which the act of reading Scripture brings us does not usually mean emotional intensity or dramatic turnabout, but rather the solemn awareness, repeated as often as daily, that the world of reality to which we have vowed ourselves in belief and vocation is a divinely constituted world in which God calls upon us; it is not a humanly constituted world in which we, when we feel like it, call upon God. Everything in the world of culture can be made sense of without God; nothing in the world of Scripture can be made sense of without God.

But the very frequency of pastoral reading in Scripture mitigates its radical strangeness in our consciousness, the crisis-conditions that are provoked in us whenever we enter its pages. But to lose that awareness is to lose our lives: we fight to stay awake. We install alarm systems around us with sensitive detection devices. Kafka rebukes our frequent and fatal regression into breezy familiarity:

> If the book we are reading does not wake us, as with a first hammering on our skull, why then do we read it? So that it

---

7. Erich Auerbach, *Mimesis* (Princeton: Princeton University Press, 1953), p. 15.

shall make us happy? Good God, we would also be happy if we had no books, and such books as make us happy we could, if need be, write ourselves. But what we must have are those books which come upon us like ill-fortune, and distress us deeply, like the death of one we love better than ourselves, like suicide. A book must be an ice axe to break the sea frozen inside us.[8]

Unable or unwilling to manage raw Scripture, pastors fall prey to a widespread practice of making it more palatable by suppressing the particularities — awkward, absurd, everyday particularities — and substituting smoothly phrased generalities. We are, after all, in the business of religion and are looking for help in raising our sights above the vulgarities of the ordinary. Particularities are wonderful in fiction, but they only get in the way of plain truth. Fiction writers are trained to render smell, sound, and feeling through specifics. The sentence "The woman felt depressed" would not occur in good fiction. Instead, the writer would describe how Gretchen cut in front of her friends while standing at the water fountain, just to the left of the elevator on the second floor, by Ethel, with whom only last night she had shared her old family recipe for moose meat chili. But Scripture isn't fiction; this is *truth,* and it ought to be rendered in two- or three-word profundities that are applicable in any situation. An abstract truth makes a wonderful poster. A generalized slogan is arresting as a bumper sticker. Isn't it the task of pastors to *interpret* Scripture, to render it in a form more in keeping with its inherent dignity?

The writers of Scripture lived in a primitive age when there was plenty of time to tell stories and elaborate details just for the fun of it. This is a different era: urgent, no-nonsense,

---

8. Quoted by George Steiner, *Language and Silence* (New York: Atheneum, 1970), p. 67.

practical. So pastors, with a lot to do, among a people with a lot to do, clear away the clutter of foreign geography and hard-to-pronounce names and boil the Bible down into Emersonian bromides manageable by goodhearted but busy people and amenable to orderly homiletic treatment. And surely, in a country that has demonstrated a decided preference for the sonorous banalities of Kahlil Gibran over the austere bluntness of St. Paul, it is hermeneutical common sense to make the rough places smooth.

Well, I have no more liking for crisis than the next pastor and would like to make things as easy as possible for both myself and my parishioners. But not easier. And here, in the reading of Scripture, the hard particularities must be fiercely guarded to prevent erosion to the bland contours of culture. Scripture is characteristically unsummarizable. It resists abstractions. It is specific, concrete, geological, genealogical. No matter that the age doesn't like this in its religious texts — pastors aren't at the beck and call of the age. What pastors must not do is extract principles from Scripture, distill truths from the gospel. Erich Auerbach has provided an extensive and powerful demonstration of the realism in the Scriptures that sets those writings apart from all other ancient literature and reshapes our perception of reality. According to him, these writers enter "into the random everyday depths of popular life," taking seriously "whatever is encountered there," clinging to the concrete and refusing to systematize experience in concepts.[9]

The great attraction for distilling Scripture into truths and morals and lessons is simply laziness. The lazy pastor no longer has to bother with the names, the cities, the odd embarrassing details and awkward miracles that refuse to fit into a modern

---

9. Auerbach, *Mimesis*, p. 44.

understanding of the good life. Across this land pastors have turned their studies into "stills," illegal distilleries that extract ideas and morals from the teeming narrative of Scripture. People, of course, love it. They come to get their Mason-jar lives filled with pure truth so that they won't have to deal with either the details of Scripture or the details of their own lives. Drinking this pure white lightning bypasses the laborious trouble of hoeing the garden, digging potatoes, preparing and cooking meals, eating and digesting. This distilled liquid goes directly to the bloodstream and gives a quick rush of exhilaration. But it is, in fact, poison. We are not constructed biologically or spiritually for ingestion of this 100-proof stuff. We have mental-emotional digestive systems with complicated interconnections that notice and savor an enormous variety of words and sentences, stories and songs, ruminatingly take them in and assimilate all the vitamins, enzymes, and calories that give us healthy lives.

The practice of distilling truths from Scripture is the hallmark of the gnostic, for whom matter is evil and history inconvenient: all the hard-edged pieces of rock and argument, the circumstantial messiness of people who are late and guests who show up early, ancestors who collected Philistine foreskins, a Messiah who launched his ministry by changing water into wine for wedding guests who had already drunk plenty (a frivolous miracle impossible to explain to serious people), and who came to his death bleeding and crying out for water, telling anyone who was still around to listen that God had abandoned him. Gnostics have no stomach for this kind of earthiness and paradox. They aspire to the spiritual and the beautiful. They go in for intricate mental constructs of how things can be reclaimed into their original sublimity, truths that are elegant with symmetries and can be arranged in "steps," lessons that are dappled with arcane profundities that

135

can be applied as "principles." The Bible, as we have it, is not to be countenanced; it must be refined. In the early Christian centuries the gnostic program was to dump the entire Hebrew Scriptures and disembowel the Gospels. The parts of St. Paul that talked theology they liked pretty well. What they pro-posed instead can be read in the documents discovered at Nag Hammadi, Egypt, in 1946:[10] Jesus as guru, safely distanced from the common and profane, serenely uttering eternal truths. This is tea-room religion where the "women come and go / Talking of Michelangelo" (T. S. Eliot).

But Scripture never comes to us this way, and the *way* it does come is as important to us as *that* it comes. Neither the crisis of Scripture nor the crisis of our lives is abstract; rather, as Marc Chagal once said, it "is a crisis of color, texture, blood and the elements of speech, vibrations, etc. — the materials with which art, like life, is constructed."[11]

> Prayer is an integral part in the study of Scripture because it anticipates the Spirit's carrying its reader through the written page to God himself.
>
> BREVARD CHILDS[12]

> The Scripture is an antecedent to our faithful lives, as faithful lives were, for those authors, an antecedent to the Scriptures.
>
> PAUL HOLMER[13]

---

10. See "Gnostic Gospels and Related Documents," in *NT Apocrypha I*, ed. E. Hennecke and W. Schneemelcher (2d ed.; 1968).

11. Quoted by Virginia Stem Owens, *And the Trees Clap Their Hands* (Grand Rapids: William B. Eerdmans, 1983), p. 89.

12. Brevard Childs, *Biblical Theology in Crisis* (Philadelphia: Westminster Press, 1970), p. 219.

13. Paul Holmer, *A Grammar of Faith* (San Francisco: Harper & Row, 1978), p. 203.

The reinterpretation of an ancient Scripture, enters into a network of intelligibility. . . . Jesus Christ himself, exegesis and exegete of Scripture, is manifested as logos in opening the understanding of the Scriptures.   PAUL RICOEUR[14]

A hermeneutically trained mind must be, from the start, sensitive to the text's quality of newness.

                              HANS-GEORG GADAMER[15]

You can't hear God speak to someone else, you can hear him only if you are being addressed.   LUDWIG WITTGENSTEIN[16]

It has seemed puzzling to me how greatly attached to the Bible you seem to be and yet how much like pagans you handle it. The great challenge to those of us who wish to take the Bible seriously is to let it teach us its own essential categories; and then for us to think *with* them, instead of just *about* them.

                              ABRAHAM HESCHEL[17]

An essay I once read gave me the image by which I have maintained ever since a clearcut awareness of what is distinctive in reading Scripture. Walker Percy wrote the essay and called it *The Message in the Bottle*.[18] He wrote it out of years of reflection

---

14. Paul Ricoeur, *Essays in Biblical Interpretation* (Philadelphia: Fortress Press, 1980), p. 52.

15. Hans-Georg Gadamer, *Truth and Method* (London: Sheed & Ward, 1975), p. 238.

16. Quoted by Anthony Thiselton, *The Two Horizons* (Grand Rapids: William B. Eerdmans, 1980), p. 386.

17. Quoted by Albert Outler, *Theology Today*, vol. 42, no. 3 (October 1985): 290.

18. Walker Percy, *The Message in the Bottle* (New York: Farrar, Straus, and Giroux, 1975).

on the nature of language and the different ways in which we use it. His essay is in the form of an extended parable. What he wrote was seminal, I take it, in shaping his own vocation as a novelist using language to tell the truth, and not just to report on the state of the nation. I am a pastor, not a novelist, and so my relation to language is not exactly parallel to his. But pastors and novelists have at least two things in common: we spend a lot of time dealing with *words;* and we believe that words are a means by which people are brought to realize the *truth about their lives.* Not all words, of course. Some words are deliberately used to distract from truth, especially when the truth is difficult or painful. Some words are used to distort the truth, especially when the distortion is marketable. And a lot of words, the majority maybe, don't seem to do much one way or the other as far as "the truth of our lives" is concerned. They are part of getting across the street, following directions for changing the furnace filter, passing a physics examination, buying broccoli. But in this welter of words, some emerge as radically different, worthy of reverence and wonder, for they tell us something otherwise inaccessible to us and reveal the truth of our lives to us.

This is the way I read the words of Scripture. At least I start out reading them this way. Most people, I think, do. But not infrequently I drift into another kind of reading. I wake myself up by asking questions: "Who cares about the culture of the Amorites? What difference does Elisha's bald head make? If Paul was so smart why is he so ambiguous?" I reflect on *this* reading and that of, say, the newspaper, two readings that I often practice back-to-back. What exactly is the difference? I never read the parts of the newspaper in which I have no personal interest (the classifieds, the stock market quotations); I regularly do it with Scripture (ceremonial legislation, oracular preaching). I never reread the newspaper the next day, even the parts that are especially well written; I continually reread Scripture the next day, even the parts that I don't think are well written (Chronicles, for instance). Walker Percy's parable-essay gave me a way to understand this difference and to guard it.

It is commonplace, I think, that without some congruence between writer and reader over the printed page there can be no understanding. A correct understanding of the words makes little difference if the minds don't meet: a recipe for bouilla-baisse cannot be read accurately as coded directions for buried treasure; a moral fable cannot be read accurately as an essay in animal husbandry; a Walker Percy novel cannot be read accurately as a gothic entertainment; and Holy Scripture cannot be read accurately as a religious textbook. In each of these instances one could plausibly read the words in the wrongheaded way I have indicated. Usually they are not — except for Scripture, which more often than not is read as a textbook on God and morals. And pastors for some reason or other are in the vanguard of these wrongheaded readers.

As I have learned from Percy's essay, I have adapted and revised it, rereading and then rewriting it as a pastor learning to read Scripture in conformance to its nature. In the process I have left out most of the subtleties in *The Message in the Bottle* and have dulled, I fear, much of the sharpness of this acutely imagined parable. But I hope Percy would not wholly disapprove of the adaption that I have made of it for my pastoral craft.

• • •
• •

Once upon a time there was an island. It was quite a large island — large enough so that its heterogeneous population could be gathered in several communities in a variety of locales with different topographies, but not so large that any part of it was not known to every other part, and all, of course, sharing the circumference of beach. The island was very pleasant and everyone seemed content to be on it. As is the case with islands, it was surrounded by what was not known. Except for small rafts and canoes that were used for fishing and sailing along the shores, no one ever left the island, or even thought to do so. All of the islanders were the descendents of castaways. But the memory of the shipwreck that put them on the island was very dim. No stories were told about it. It was not recorded in the histories. Officially it was denied, for it would seem to detract from the desirability and completeness of the place.

These islanders were a curious and intelligent people. They had identified, studied, and classified all the plants and animals. They had examined the rocks and mapped the hills and streams. They knew the names and nesting places of all the birds. They were familiar with the mating rituals of the mammals and the care they gave their young. They knew when the flowers bloomed and for how long, which nuts were good for eating, which roots had medicinal properties. The land that was beneath their feet was appreciated and understood — *named.* It gave them a deep sense of orientation and satisfaction to know what to call everything that they saw.

In the course of doing this they had also been careful to pass on this knowledge from generation to generation. They had learned how to teach young minds to comprehend what their elders understood. Their school system was wonderful: they talked in explanatory and guiding ways so that there was no slippage between youthful ignorance and mature knowledge. Developing language for this purpose was a great achievement, for it involved subtleties far exceeding those in distinguishing varieties of sparrows — they had to take into account feelings, the slow and uncertain growth of ideas, the expression of hard-to-convey attitudes. But they did it. There was no generation gap on the island. They exercised great skill in talking to each other about what they knew about the world and in using these conversations to draw the growing capacities for language in the young up to the level of their elders.

They were also good at using this language with each other — wives with husbands, employers with employees, brothers with sisters. Even with all the complications of authority, love, and rivalry there were no misunderstandings, ever, on the island. They were able to say exactly what they wanted to say, and to hear accurately what was said. There were, of course, squabbles and fights from time to time, people being what they are, but that was because they didn't *agree* on something. No one was ever heard to walk away from these spats saying, "She just doesn't understand me" or "Why *won't* he understand?" They held no seminars for improving communication skills. They had that part down.

This expertise in language reached its most impressive demonstration in their political and community discourse. They had a constitution and other public documents that everyone understood: vast areas of experience and social relationships were summarized in words and phrases so that everyone had a pretty good idea of what was going on. They were able to talk about large subjects like justice, virtue, peace, and even happiness, and each know what the other was talking about. When the developing maturity of the population required some alteration in their community expectations or perceptions, they were able to enact that legislatively in words that expressed a consensus of the wise perceptions of the community. Occasionally they got together and celebrated these verbal formulations in parades and picnics.

It was a pretty nice island, especially if you cared about language. The scientists seemed to be on top of everything that was going on and described it accurately. The schools were a delight to be in, with teachers and students in friendly and leisurely dialogue. Families understood each other even when they didn't like each other. If you listened in on conversations and discussions that took place in government chambers and business boardrooms, the clarity and elegance with which language was spoken was impressive.

(One of the striking omissions of word-usage on the island was for advertising and public relations. Curious: among this people who communicated so well there was no communication industry. Since everything was well identified and there was open, honest, and accurate transaction of information at every level of society, there was apparently no need for anyone to say anything in other than a normal tone of voice in the natural course of an encounter. As a result, while words were used extremely well, they were not used nearly as often, and so the practice of language included a great deal more silence than non-island people experience.)

One day, down on the beach, a green bottle rode in on the crest of a wave and landed on the sand. An islander was there and picked it up. He noticed a piece of paper inside, took it out, and read, "Help is coming." Strange. He had never read or heard anything like it. All his needs were taken care of. The island-world was completely and happily self-sufficient. He had never supposed that he needed help. All the same, the three-word message touched some level of awareness in him he had no name for. He was intrigued. He looked across the horizon, as bland and featureless as always, and saw nothing different. He stuffed the biodegradable paper in the sand, threw the bottle into a recycling barrel at the edge of a dune, walked home, and said nothing about it to anybody. A few weeks later, walking on the same beach, the man picked up another bottle. There was a message in this bottle also. It read, "Help will arrive soon, don't give up." Twice is not an accident. He told a friend. They went to the beach together. They had long enjoyed the feel of the sand, the curve and color of the shells, the sounding rhythmic waves; but now they found themselves looking for bottles. Occasionally they would find one, as always with the absurd message: "Help left yesterday"; "Take heart, help will certainly come." Absurd, because they didn't *need* help. And yet morning after morning they were there, looking, reading those message fragments that were telling them something that they had never known they wanted to hear. Word got around. On Sunday mornings especially there would be quite a gathering of people on the beach, attentive to the waves, wondering if the next swell would bring a bottle with a message in it. Weeks would go by without a bottle, and then two or three would be washed up together.

Most people couldn't see what the excitement was about. With an island full of well-written books, carefully edited dictionaries, and clearly written handbooks, they had information and explanations for everything that they had ever seen and had to deal with. Why would anyone stand around on a chilly beach in the morning hoping for a cryptic message that wasn't *about* anything?

But those who met on the beach shared a hard-to-describe curiosity and wonder that was new to them in the use of language. Words were being used in these bottle messages in ways they had never experienced — to show not what was there but what was not there. Someone was saying something they didn't understand and taking no particular pains to explain or inform or convince. Curiously, this use of language in a way they didn't understand exercised a pull on them stronger than the language they did understand. Wasn't language the most rational of human activities? How could it so effectively hold their attention when it wasn't making them understand? They weren't *learning* anything from the messages. They were being addressed by an unknown someone who was telling them something they didn't know they needed. The world was larger, far larger apparently, than anything for which their language had ever provided evidence. And maybe their lives were larger than the island language was giving expression to. That was what drew them back to the beach those mornings and held their attention to the ritualized waves against the enigmatic horizon. The messages in the bottles had stirred something in them they hadn't known was there — a sense that there might be a lot more to life than the island language had expressed, that there was more outside the island than inside it. From across those seas, someone was saying something to them that sounded like the difference between life and death, or at least between being helped and being helpless. They wanted to know as much about it as possible.

The strange scrawls gathered power over them and came to mean more to them than all the books and memos and bulletins that kept their island communications system working with such flawless efficiency.

But it is the nature of *these* words to tell us not what is here, but what is not here — at least what we have not yet recognized as here. It is the genius of these words to bring us a message from beyond the limits of our understanding, not to improve our communication systems. It is the character of these words to reach from beyond the horizons of our capacity and invade what we had supposed was a self-sufficient island of discourse.

It hardly matters that the message is fragmentary.

It hardly matters that we can't figure out all the referents.

It hardly matters that we can't organize it into something systematically complete.

What matters is that it links us with a larger world, perhaps a *main*land.

144

What matters is that it announces help in getting out of a mere island (I-land) existence — efficient, smooth, scientific, harmonious — in which the self knows everything but its self. And its God.

What I must not do is take the message in the bottle and enter it in the card catalogue of the library. What I must not do is take the message out of the bottle and study the bottle, analyze its chemical makeup, and reconstruct the glassblowing technique that shaped it. What I must not do is reductively compare the message in the bottle with the concise island memos, and condescendingly rewrite it because it "doesn't communicate very well."

Most mornings on the island on many of its beaches there are people walking, wonderingly attentive, looking for bottles with a message in them. On Sunday mornings they gather on some assigned beaches and read to each other what has been collected over the years. A lot of people on the island have yet to figure out what all the fuss is about.

Third Angle

SPIRITUAL
DIRECTION

VII

Being a Spiritual Director

THE CULTURE conditions us to approach people and situations as journalists: see the big, exploit the crisis, edit and abridge the commonplace, interview the glamorous. But the Scriptures and our best pastoral traditions train us in a different approach: notice the small, persevere in the commonplace, appreciate the obscure.

Erich Auerbach in his wonderful book *Mimesis* saw the significance of the Christian faith as "the birth of a spiritual movement in the depths of the common people, from within the everyday occurrences of contemporary life. . . ."[1] He went on to contrast the Christian movement with the original Roman conquest: "The agents of Christianity do not simply organize an administration from above, leaving everything else to its natural development; they are duty bound to take an interest in the specific detail of everyday incidents; Christianization is directly concerned with and concerns the individual person and the individual event."[2]

---

1. Erich Auerbach, *Mimesis* (Princeton: Princeton University Press, 1953), p. 43.

2. Ibid., p. 92.

Spiritual direction is the aspect of ministry that explores and develops this absorbing and devout attentiveness to "the specific detail of everyday incidents," "the everyday occurrences of contemporary life." It counters and resists the pressure to shape pastoral work on the pattern of the "Roman conquest."

Spiritual direction is the task of helping a person take seriously what is treated dismissively by the publicity-infatuated and crisis-sated mind, and then to receive this "mixed, random material of life" (Auerbach's words again) as the raw material for high holiness.

Spiritual direction takes place when two people agree to give their full attention to what God is doing in one (or both) of their lives and seek to respond in faith. More often than not for pastors these convergent and devout attentions are brief and unplanned; at other times they are planned and structured conversations. Whether planned or unplanned, three convictions underpin these meetings: (1) God is always doing something: an active grace is shaping this life into a mature salvation; (2) responding to God is not sheer guesswork: the Christian community has acquired wisdom through the centuries that provides guidance; (3) each soul is unique: no wisdom can simply be applied without discerning the particulars of this life, this situation.

I have been talking with friends and colleagues for several years now about spiritual direction. Many are unfamiliar with the term and uneasy with its implications. Most don't think they are qualified for it. Yet when we talk of what they are actually doing, a surprising amount of it is spiritual direction. But almost always there is also this: what I call spiritual direction is what they are doing when they don't think they are doing anything

important. It is what takes place in the corners, in the unscheduled parts of their day. It is offhand. And they do less of
it than they otherwise might because they are so tightly
scheduled or so intently involved in completing a task or a
project. I think that a lot of pastors would do it a lot more,
both more consistently and more skillfully, if they realized how
much more important it is than our teachers ever told us, and
how large a place in pastoral ministry it always filled in earlier
centuries.

It turns out that no one I talk to deliberately rejects the
work of spiritual direction, nor goes very long without engaging
in it somehow or other. Still, by and large it is a fringe activity
for most. Being a spiritual director, which used to loom large
at the center of every pastor's common work, in our times has
been pushed to the periphery of ministry.

Ironically, this is the work that many people assume that
pastors do all the time: teaching people to pray, helping parishioners discern the presence of grace in events and feelings,
affirming the presence of God at the very heart of life, sharing
a search for light through a dark passage in the pilgrimage,
guiding the formation of a self-understanding that is biblically
spiritual instead of merely psychological or sociological.

But pastors don't do it all the time or nearly enough of
the time. Some don't do it very often because they don't have
time for it, or don't think they have time for it, which amounts
to the same thing. Others slight it because they have no idea
of how important it is. Whenever it is done, though, there is
an instinctive recognition that this work is at the very center
of the pastoral vocation.

Spiritual direction means taking seriously, with a disciplined attention and imagination, what others take casually.
"Pray for me" is often a casual remark. The spiritual director
gives it full attention. All those moments in life when awareness

151

of God breaks through the crust of our routines — a burst of praise, a pang of guilt, an episode of doubt, boredom in worship — these take place all the time and are mentioned from time to time in half-serious ways while we are on the run to something big or important. Being a spiritual director means a readiness to clear space and arrange time to look at these elements of our life that are not at all peripheral but are central — unobtrusive signals of transcendance. By naming and attending and conversing, we teach our friends to "read the Spirit" and not just the newspapers.

A friend did this for me recently. I had returned to my parish after several weeks away. One of the elders met me and said, "Weeds have sprouted in the garden while you were gone." He gave details: carping criticism about little things, fault-finding remarks about me — nothing substantial but the kind of thing that can develop into an atmosphere of suspicious, distrustful unrest. I was hurt and disappointed. And then I was angry. Everything had been working smoothly when I left. Now a handful of people with some careless and perhaps malicious talk had put things in commotion. The elder advised me to take care of things immediately to preserve the peace and unity of the church. Confront, explain, smooth over, do a little cheerleading along the way. He didn't want me or my ministry to be misrepresented. And he didn't want the church's life disrupted. I agreed. I made plans to smooth the waters. At this point a friend introduced spiritual direction into the action. He asked me to sum up what was going on. That was easy: I was angry over what had been said about me personally and I was concerned about the seeds of dissent in the congregation. And what was I going to do about it? I was going to confront the people who were criticizing me behind my back and force them to deal with me face-to-face. And I would rebuild the peace of the congregation through visitation and preaching. Actually, it was routine pastoral work. He interrupted my conventional approach. "Don't you think there might be more to your anger than righteous indignation? Don't you think it could be a symptom of pride that you didn't know you had? Why don't you explore the dimensions and ramifications of your anger? And as to the unrest; what if the Spirit is preparing something new in the congregation? What if the whitecaps on the recently smooth waters are caused by the wind of the Spirit, not the whispers of critics? Isn't it possible that you are working for a premature and bland peace when something deeply creative is in motion?" He named the anger as sin; he discerned the unrest as Spirit. He directed me to the essential work of dealing with my sin and responding to the Spirit. The things I had set out to do still had to be done, but they were mere footnotes to the major work that he set before me. He directed me to the obvious, but in my passion to clear myself and to have a smilingly harmonious congregation I hadn't so much as noticed the obvious. That is why the work of spiritual direction is essential — because we need to deal with the obvious, with sin and with the Spirit, and we would rather deal with almost anything else.

In these moments when we are in conversation with another and spirit touches spirit, "deep calling to deep," there is often a confirming sense that we are doing our best work. So we don't need to be talked into doing this, at least most of us do not. For most pastors being a spiritual director doesn't mean introducing a new rule or adding another item to our overextended job descriptions, but simply rearranging our perspective: seeing certain acts as eternal and not ephemeral, as essential and not accidental. Spiritual directors used to be important because they attended to what everyone agreed was important; they are important now because they are about the only people left who confirm the insights and longings that everyone in fugitive moments thinks might be important, but

153

that get brushed aside by urgent and hurrying experts on their way to a therapy session or a committee meeting. There are so many other things clamoring for attention that these timidly voiced, apologetically phrased needs and longings get by-passed. The spiritual director is in charge of attending to these quiet necessities.

I was meeting with my friend Tom, a pastor in a nearby town. At mid-morning we walked across the street to a diner for a cup of coffee. I went to the washroom and on returning found Tom in earnest conversation with the waitress. I delayed my return by picking up a newspaper and looking through it so as not to interrupt them. The conversation lasted perhaps three minutes. When I was back at the table and we were finishing our coffee I commented on the appearance of intensity in both of them. Tom was wistful as he talked about how often this waitress evoked the best in him by her questions and interest in God. Then he said, "I wish I could spend a lot more time at this sort of thing. I sometimes have the feeling that I am more of a pastor in this diner than I ever am in my church study." I asked him, "Why on earth then don't you do it more?" He looked at me in a kind of surprise: "Where would I get the time? And besides, that is not what they are paying me to do, is it?"

That seems to me outrageously wrong — that Tom should acquiesce to a view of what he is getting paid for that prevents him from engaging in what pastors have always been expected to practice. Too much spiritual direction is off-the-cuff work. Too many pastors only dabble in spiritual direction.

$$\bullet \ \bullet \ \bullet$$
$$\bullet \ \bullet \ \bullet$$

But a recovery is underway. More and more pastors are seizing this old identity and making it their own, refusing any longer to let it be marginal to their ministries. The basic requirement for being a spiritual director is simply to take seriously what we already know are serious matters — a sign of grace here, a desire for prayer there — and shape the agenda of our work from the souls of people we meet, not from the demands to which they give voice.

The difficulty in taking these kinds of things seriously is that we inhabit an atmosphere so full of rush and demand. Pastors practice their craft in the middle of a traffic jam, noisy with people's hurts, dangerous with hurtling ambitions and reckless urgencies, crowded with people intent on getting to their destinations and angrily frustrated when others are impediments in their path. Pastors are not Indian gurus sitting quietly in an ashram receiving people who come hundreds and thousands of miles to observe them in postures of sanctity. Nothing in our culture and little in our churches encourages us in the work of spiritual direction. If being a spiritual director is going to be something more than a wistfully procrastinated intention it will only be by consciously opposing the "principalities and powers of the air."

A simple act of naming is part of the recovery. "Spiritual direction" is not the only term adequate to describe this work, and I don't insist on it. Nor is the naming essential for everyone. No doubt a significant number of pastors have never been diverted from this central work and have never so much as heard of spiritual direction or any of its synonyms.

Nevertheless, naming is important. What is unnamed is often unnoticed. Naming focuses attention. The precise name confers dignity. My most memorable experience of this came in naming birds. I have known what a bird was from an early age and could name a few of them — robin, crow, sparrow. The ones I named I noticed (not the other way around). I was aware that birds were in the air and bushes and trees but never paid much attention to them. Then I became a bird-watcher.

I learned to observe the birds, not just to glance at them. Within a few weeks I was seeing an enormous variety of birds and noticing how extraordinarily different they were from each other. And I began to be in awe of how much there was yet to know, and how long a lifetime I would need to arrive at a mastery, and to regret my late start. A new world had opened up right before my eyes: colors, sounds, flight patterns. But it had always been there. Why was I now seeing? In large part through naming. Without a taxonomy, a science of naming, I would neither notice nor remember the red-eyed vireo, towhee, Baltimore oriole, winter wren, Lewis woodpecker.

Warren had arranged to talk with me. He wasn't himself experiencing what he observed in others in the Christian life. He had kept quiet about it for a long time, thinking there must be something wrong with him. He felt flat and uninteresting. There was no inward zest. When others talked of grace, mercy, joy, and peace in Christ, he felt left out. He told me about himself. I learned something he had told no one else, that there was a major relationship in his life that was extremely unfortunate. He had decided that he would simply live with it, try not to feel sorry for himself, and get on as best he could. He had concluded that the other person in the relationship was emotionally sick and that improvement could not be hoped for — still he couldn't quit hoping. He would be courageous in hoping. I listened. I listened some more. We prayed. After several weeks I ventured: "You have named this person 'sick.' That implies that no one is responsible, but if we try hard enough we might find a medicine or therapy that will make him better. What if we named his influence 'envy'? That means that there is an actively malicious will at work. You have named your part in this as 'courage.' What if we named it 'sloth,' meaning that you are too lazy to enter into the hard work of prayer in a spiritual warfare?" Clarification was immediate. By a simple act of naming, he discerned the reality of his life.

Emotional deprivation did not cause the flatness in his life; a malign will had enervated his spirit. With continuing direction and encouragement he gave up the fight against "flesh and blood" and took up the battle against the "principalities" and the "powers" (Eph. 6:12) and gradually began to know within himself the meaning of grace, mercy, joy, and peace in Christ.

Being a spiritual director means noticing the familiar, naming the particular. Being knowledgeable in the large truths of sin, grace, salvation, atonement, and judgment is necessary but not sufficient. A lot of our work takes place in the details of the particular. It is the difference between being vaguely aware that birds are everywhere and naming particular birds. Every temptation has a different look and nuance. Every grace has its own ambience and angle of refraction. In spiritual direction we don't apply truth so much as discover particular temptations and actual graces. Casual and perfunctory habits of judging and labeling give way to the energies of a disciplined imagination and a prayerful attentiveness.

The naming for me brought clarity in matters that were badly blurred. I had grown up in a tradition that categorized all discussion of the practice of prayer and discernment and any effort to recognize the presence of God and direct the formation of mature faith with the labels "devotional help" and "inspirational aid." Anyone who had anything helpful to say of a guiding or encouraging nature was lumped in the devotional/inspirational bin. A lot of people, it turns out, have spiritual advice to give to their brothers and sisters in the faith. Any uplifting experience acquired while playing in the last ten minutes of a football game or while changing a diaper, any devout thought that occurs while taking a morning shower qualifies as a text. Sheer sincerity, undisfigured by the scars of wisdom, confers authority to speak or write with, as they say, "all the rights and privileges pertaining thereunto." A winning smile is widely held to compensate adequately for the inability to write. Exclamation marks, liberally inserted, cover a multitude of syntactical deficiencies. Cutely sentimental stories pretending to show a pursuit after holiness are embarrassing parodies of it. When sincerity and sentimentality meet, "devotional helps" and "inspirational aids" spring into being.

I read dozens of these books, hoping to learn about prayer and the "feel" of faith, to get an orientation in the shadowed complexities of the soul's journey. Finally, though, I became bored with the third-rate writing and disgusted by the platitudinous dishonesties. I went looking for stronger meat in theology, history, and Hebrew and Greek exegesis. I adopted a pose of dismissive condescension toward the inspirational and devotional. But the longing for direction was still there. The hunger for companionship wouldn't go away. I shelved but did not quite abandon hope for matters in the spiritual life, for mentors in prayer, for experienced companions in the soul's itinerary.

And then I began to find them, one by one, here and there. In obscure corners of libraries far from the best-seller racks. In quiet, easy-to-overlook persons well out of the promotional limelight. I read. I listened. I discovered people who were at the same time sane and devout, disciplined and mature, intelligent and wise. There were not many of them, but they were most certainly *there*. These people brought a fierce intelligence, a disciplined moral imagination, and a well-tested spiritual maturity to matters of God and the soul. They were dealing with the questions that I raised whenever I was moving into the heart of the faith, struggling to find my personal way through the difficulties of Scripture or the mysteries of prayer or the "dark night of the soul."

I was delighted to find large-souled men and women thinking strenuously and living arduously at the deep center of life. But I was also surprised: why had no professor so much as mentioned the subject of spiritual direction? Why had no pastor ever showed more than a touristy interest when I tried to give voice to my heart? And later why did no one tell me that the essential work in which I would be occupied as a pastor had this rich tradition of practice and learning, and that I must be acquainted with it? They were careful enough that I learn Scripture and theology; why did they keep this away from me? Why had no one given me a bird book and a pair of binoculars? Was it ignorance or indifference? I'll never know.

A few years ago a learned journal devoted an issue to celebrating the achievements of a leading pastoral theologian of our time, a professor who influenced the shape of ministry probably as much as any other in the American church. Of all the articles written in tribute not one mentioned prayer or spiritual direction. I went to the professor's books, all of which I own, and went through the indexes — not a single entry on prayer or spiritual direction. This from a man who is teaching us to be *pastors?* The assumption, no doubt, is that you learn these things at your mother's knee, or in Sunday school; it is not the sort of thing to which one gives graduate-school attention, for heaven's sake.

∴ ∴

Nicholas Berdyaev clarifies the grounds for spiritual direction in this sentence: "In a certain sense, every single human soul has more meaning and value than the whole of history with its empires, its wars and revolutions, its blossoming and fading civilizations."[3] But who is there to insist on this meaning and

---

3. Nicholas Berdyaev, *The Fate of Man in the Modern World* (Ann Arbor: University of Michigan Press, 1969), p. 12.

value in a world craving for generalizations and dealing in commodities? I'm voting for pastors who in the midst of their other duties take up the work of spiritual direction.

Any Christian can do this, and many do. Spiritual direction is no prerogative of the ordained ministry. Some of the best spiritual directors are simply friends. Some of the most famous spiritual directors have been laypersons. But the fact that anybody can do it and that it can occur at any time and place must not be construed to mean that it can be done casually or indifferently. It needs to be practiced out of a life immersed in the pursuit of holiness.

What is required is that we bring the same disciplined prayer and discerning attentiveness into the commonplaces that we bring to the preparation of lectures and sermons, sharing crises of illness and death, celebrating births and marriages, launching campaigns and stirring up visions. It means putting the full spotlight of prayerful concern on the parts of life that get no other spotlights put on them. Being a spiritual director is bringing the same care and skill and intensity to the ordinary, boring, uneventful parts of our lives that we readily give to the eventful conversions and proclamations.

Most spiritual direction takes place spontaneously and informally in unplanned but "just right" moments. I have been given spiritual direction by persons who didn't know they were giving it while waiting at a red light, while climbing a mountain, while interrupting an assigned task with a coffee break. In retrospect it is impressive how critically formative these unimportant, unscheduled, squeezed-in exchanges have turned out to be.

Occasionally this gets formalized: conversations are arranged in which two people seek companionship, encouragement, and insight in pursuing the life of prayer, developing an integrated and mature life of faith, maintaining an attentive alertness to God's action at all times and in everything. But except for those who are set apart vocationally to provide spiritual direction in communities or schools, formalized direction will not be what pastors do most. For me, at least, formal spiritual direction involves only five or six people with whom I meet at intervals of four to six weeks.

Meanwhile the informal aspects of spiritual direction are there all the time for pastors. C. S. Lewis described us as "those particular people within the whole church who have been especially set aside to look after what concerns us as creatures who are going to live forever."[4] People want more in faith, in life, in God. It is not unreasonable that they should look for direction from their pastors. And they don't wait until we enter our pulpits to look at and listen to us. Beyond the boundaries of our awareness, who we are and what we say may be critical for anyone at any moment. As much by inadvertence as by design, we make a difference. Realizing this motivates us to learn the disciplines of spiritual direction. We prayerfully cultivate an awareness that God has designs on this person, that God is acting in this situation, that God is bringing some purpose long in process to fulfillment right now.

This is one part of our work that stubbornly resists generalizations. All the same, I will risk one: the "unimportant" parts of ministry might be the most important. The things that we do when we don't think we are doing anything significant might make the most difference. It is certainly true in my own life that the people who have helped me most weren't trying to help me and didn't know they were helping when they were. Conversely, the people who tried hardest to help were often no help at all. The ones who took me on as a project made the faith more difficult and not infrequently introduced

---

4. C. S. Lewis, *Mere Christianity* (New York: Macmillan, 1976), p. 97.

obstacles into my life that it took years to get through or around.

By its very nature — obscure, everyday, low profile, non-crisis — this is the work for which we need the most encouragement if we are to keep it at the center of our awareness and practice. It is in fact the work for which we get the least encouragement, for it is always being pushed to the sidelines by the hustling, career-development mentality of our peers and by the hurrying, stimulus-hunger demands of our parishioners.

: : :
: : :

Our slowness to engage in the unglamorous, obscure work of spiritual direction is not new. The more public, exhortational, motivational aspects of ministry have always been more attractive. In the first century St. Paul observed, "Though you have countless guides in Christ, you do not have many fathers" (1 Cor. 4:15). It is easier to tell people what to do than to be with them in a discerning, prayerful companionship as they work it out. The unfavorable ratio of "guides" to "fathers" doesn't seem to have changed in twenty centuries. If anything it is aggravated by the mass marketing of spiritual helps. People looking for guidance get paperback best-sellers, digest articles, television talk show guests. But the very nature of the life of faith requires the personal and the immediate if we are going to mature: not only wisdom but a wise person to understand *us* in relation to the wisdom. A person in need and in growth is vulnerable and readily accepts counsel that is sincerely given. But the help that might be right for someone else, even right for this person at another time, can be wrong for this person at this time. So the congregation's need for personal spiritual direction cannot be delegated to books or tapes or videos. It is the pastor's proper work.

There are as many different ways of engaging in this work as there are shapes of snowflakes and kinds of flowers. Our individuality and the individuality of the other increase in these encounters and meetings so that it is impossible to predetermine what should be done or said. But there is a basic stance that we take. It would be unwise to forget for a moment that in this business we are sinners dealing with sinners; still, the primary orientation is toward God, looking for grace. It is easier to look for sin. The variants of error are finite. The "deadly sins" can be numbered; it is virtue that exhibits the endless fertility of creation.

A favorite theme of C. S. Lewis was that "heaven will show much more variety than hell." All our mistakes turn out to have a sameness about them. There is nothing quite as unoriginal as sin. But as we cultivate the practice of spiritual direction we find ourselves working in a field where the Spirit is inventive and the forms of grace are not repeated. In George Eliot's fine observation, we "discern that the mysterious complexity of our life is not to be embraced by maxims, and that to lace ourselves up in formulas of that sort is to repress all the divine promptings and inspirations that spring from growing insight and sympathy."[5]

---

5. George Eliot, *The Mill on the Floss* (New York: Century, 1911), p. 310.

VIII

Getting a Spiritual Director

THERE IS A saying among physicians that the doctor who is his own doctor has a fool for a doctor. It means, as I understand it, that the care of the body is a complex business and requires cool, detached judgment. We not only have bodies, we *are* bodies, and so none of us is capable of untainted objectivity regarding our own bodies. All of us, physicians included, want coddling, not healing. We prefer comfort to wholeness. And we can deceive ourselves about ourselves endlessly.

If those entrusted with the care of the body cannot be trusted to look after their own bodies, far less can those entrusted with the care of souls look after their own souls, which are even more complex than bodies and have a correspondingly greater capacity for self-deceit.

For a long time in the church's life, people expected that the pastor, one entrusted to give personal and detailed guidance to people journeying and growing in the way of faith, would be provided with an equivalent guidance. Having a spiritual director, whether called by that name or not, was assumed in the job description.[1] But not any more. It is rare today to find a pastor who has a spiritual director.

This widespread loss of what in healthier times was assumed leaves the pastor in enormous, though usually unnoticed, peril. And the wreckage accumulates: we find pastors who don't pray, pastors who don't grow in faith, pastors who can't tell the difference between culture and the Christ, pastors who chase fads, pastors who are cynical and shopworn, pastors who know less about prayer after twenty years of praying than they did on the day of their ordination, pastors with arrogant, outsized egos puffed up by years of hot-air flattery from well-meaning parishioners: "Great sermon, Pastor. . . . Wonderful prayer, Pastor. . . . I couldn't have made it through without you, Pastor. . . ."

---

1. St. Dorotheus of Gaza is representative of this consensus:

There is nothing more harmful than trying to direct oneself. . . . That's why I never allowed myself to follow my own desires without seeking counsel. . . . In the Book of Proverbs it says, "Those who have no guidance fall like leaves but there is security in good advice" (11:14). Take a clear look at this saying brothers. Look at what Scripture teaches us. It tells us that we should not establish ourselves as guides, that we should not consider ourselves wise, that we should not ever think we can direct ourselves. We need another's help; we need guidance besides God's grace. No one is poorer, no one is more defenseless than a person who has no one to guide him along the road to God. Scripture says, "Those who have no guidance fall like leaves." Leaves are always green at the start; they grow quickly and are quite pleasing to look at. Then, after awhile, they dry up and drop off, and in the end, they are blown about by the wind and are walked on. So is the person who is not guided by someone. At first, he has great fervor about fasting, keeping prayerful watch, silence, obedience, and other ascetic practices. After a short time, the fire is put out, and not having anyone to guide him and support him, and kindle his fire again, he dries up, and so, becoming disobedient he falls and finally becomes a tool in the hand of his enemies, who do what they want to with him.

Quoted in *Writings on Spiritual Direction*, ed. Jerome M. Neufelder and Mary C. Coelho (New York: Seabury Press, 1982), p. 3.

The position of authority is a perilous one. At memorable moments of life — baptism, confirmation, marriage, reconciliation, death — pastors are robed in dignity and represent God's authority. We proclaim the authoritative word of God at pulpit, table, and font. All sorts and conditions of people come to us and listen to the definitive word of God spoken from our mouths. They expose the sins and hurts of their guilty lives, trusting to our wise discernment. They look up to us as persons in authority.

But the practice of our faith involves the exact opposite of wielding authority, namely, the exercise of obedience. Faith is an act of submission to the Lordship of Christ, a willing response to his commands. However much our pastoral office requires that we speak and act authoritatively in the name of our Lord, our Christian identity consists in being a servant. Paul, characteristically, pushed that identity as far as it would go — slave (*doulos*). But if we are exercising authority all the time, when do we have a chance to practice obedience?

Our position requires that we act with authority; our faith requires that we live in submission. While we are busy passing out the Lord's commands in our congregations and communities, who is there to represent the same authority to us? Our already healthy propensity for pride is goaded a dozen times a day with no one in sight to check it. It is not merely nice for pastors to have a spiritual director; it is indispensable:

> Everybody should know this truth that no one is gifted with such prudence and wisdom as to be adequate for himself in the guidance of his own spiritual life. Self-love is a blind guide and fools many. The light of our own judgment is weak and we cannot envision all dangers or snares and errors to which we are prone in the life of the spirit.[2]

---

2. John Cardinal Bona, *A Treatise of Spiritual Life,* trans. D. A. Donovan (New York: Pustet, 1901), pp. 5, 66.

In the best of all possible worlds, no pastor would "get" a spiritual director. We would already have one — not by our choice or inclination, but by assignment. For the very act of choosing a spiritual director for ourselves can defeat the very thing we are after. If we avoid anyone who we sense will not be tenderly sympathetic to the "dearest idols we have known" and opt for conversational coziness, we have only doubled our jeopardy. But we don't live in the best of all possible worlds, in which someone looks after us in these matters, and the vocational/spiritual peril in which the pastor lives is so acute that, dangerous or not (but very mindful of the danger), pastors must get spiritual directors. Our spiritual sanity requires it.

For myself, getting a spiritual director meant overcoming a lifetime bias against anyone who would exercise spiritual authority over me. I listened to my elders, of course — pastors and teachers — but always on my terms: I selected what suited me and rejected the rest.

From Isaiah's Mt. Zion, to Dante's Mt. Purgatory, to St. John of the Cross's ascent of Mt. Carmel, climbing a mountain has been a metaphor for the developing life of faith. Most experienced climbers, faced with a high and difficult mountain, rope themselves together for their ascent. There is a skilled lead climber; if someone falls there is a linked safety system. But some climbers set out on their own. They bushwhack through the underbrush, laboriously figure out each difficulty on the mountain with guidebook, map, compass, and a lot of trial and error. These climbers also gain the summit, but the accidents and fatalities among them are far more frequent. On the lower slopes of the mountain, it never occurred to me to have a guide. But about halfway up the mountain, alarmed at how many maimed and dead bodies of other pastors I was seeing, I became frightened. Aware of the danger of the enterprise and my own ignorance of the mountain, I decided that I must have a skilled guide, a spiritual director. The way I did it can best be set out, I think, in a representative anecdote.

Twenty-five years ago in Baltimore I heard Pete Seeger play the five-string banjo. I was seized with the conviction that I must do it too. I was in graduate school at Johns Hopkins University at the time and had little money, but poverty was no deterrent in the rush of such urgencies: I went to the pawn shops on East Baltimore Street the next morning and bought a banjo for eleven dollars. I found an instruction manual in a used-book store for fifty cents. I was on my way. I applied myself to strumming and flailing and three-finger picking. I had neither the time nor the money for formal instruction, but in odd moments between seminars and papers I worked at making the sounds and singing the songs that Seeger had introduced into my life. In the years following, the impetus of the first enthusiasm slackened. I repeated myself a lot. From time to time I would pick up another instruction book, another songbook.

Occasionally someone would be in our home who played the banjo and I would pick up a new technique. At such moments I became fleetingly aware of a great pool of lore that banjo players took for granted. I recognized some of the items from the footnotes and appendices in my instruction books. Eventually I realized that if I was going to advance, I would have to get a teacher. It wasn't that I lacked knowledge — my stack of instruction books was now quite high. It wasn't that I lacked material — there were already far more songs in my books than I could ever learn well. But I didn't seem to be able to get the hang of it by just reading about them.

I have not yet hired a teacher. It was never the right time. I procrastinated. I am still picking and singing the same songs I learned in the first few years. The crisp, glittering banjo sound that never failed to set feet tapping and laughter rippling now bores my wife and children to tears. I am not a little bored myself. I still intend to get a teacher.

: : :
: : :

A desire for prayer was kindled in me early in life. When the embers cooled, as they did from time to time, I applied the bellows of a lecture or a book or a workshop or a conference. The evangelical movement, in which I grew up, gave frequent exhortations to pray. I was told in many and various ways that prayer was urgent. There was also a great quantity of didactic material on prayer, most of it in books. I responded to the exhortations and read the books. But useful as these resources were to get me started and established, there came a time when I felt the need for something else — something more personal, more intimate.

But what? As I groped for clarity in what I wanted I found out what I did not want. I didn't want a counselor or therapist. I was not conscious of any incapacitating neurosis that needed fixing. I did not want information; I already knew far more than I practiced. It was not for lack of knowledge that I was unsettled. And it wasn't exactly a friend that I wanted, a person with whom I could unburden my inner hopes and fears when I felt like it.

My sense of need was vague and unfocused. It had, though, to do with my development in prayer and my growth in faith — I knew that much. It also had to do with what Francis de Sales called "the ambushes and deceits of the wicked one."[3] But I didn't know how to get it. I began to pray for someone who would guide me in the essential, formative parts

---

3. Francis de Sales, *Introduction to the Devout Life,* trans. John K. Ryan (Garden City, NY: Doubleday & Co., 1955), p. 42.

of my life: my sense of God, my practice of prayer, my understanding of grace. I wanted someone who would take my life of prayer and my pilgrimage with Christ as seriously (or more seriously) than I did, who was capable of shutting up long enough to hear the distinct uniqueness of my spirituality, and who had enough disciplined restraint not to impose an outside form on me.

I knew from my books that in previous centuries spiritual directors were a regular part of the life of faith. I also knew that in other traditions it was unthinkable for persons who had any kind of leadership responsibilities in the life of prayer to proceed without a spiritual director. Spiritual intensities were dangerous and the heart desperately wicked: anyone entering the lion's cage of prayer required regular, personal guidance. But this knowledge, like the footnotes and appendices in my banjo books, was outside the orbit of my associations and experience.

Besides, I like doing things on my own. Figuring them out. Mastering skills. Fasting. Double-thumbing. Meditating. It was all right for a person who was uninstructed or unmotivated to get help, but I was neither. "Just Jesus and me" was deeply embedded in my understanding of the mature Christian life. The goal was independence from every human relationship and intimacy with Christ alone.

All the same, going against the grain of training and inclination, I found myself with a focused prayer: "Lead me to a spiritual director." I considered various friends and acquaintances. Somehow no one seemed right. I sensed that they would not understand my needs. I may have been wrong in this — in one instance I know now that I was. But no one seemed to be the answer to my prayer for a spiritual director.

I was in no real hurry. I kept alert. In the course of this waiting and watching I met a man whom I gradually came to feel was the person who could be my spiritual director. The more I knew him the more confident I became that he would understand me and guide me wisely.

At this point I greatly surprised myself: I didn't ask him. I was convinced that I needed a spiritual director. I was reasonably sure this person would be a good director for me. And suddenly I felt this great reluctance to approach him. We were quite regularly together and so I had frequent opportunities to approach him. But I procrastinated.

It didn't take me long to get to the root of my reluctance: I didn't want to share what was most essential to me. I wanted to keep control. I wanted to be boss. I had often felt and sometimes complained of the loneliness of prayer, but now I found unconsciously cherished pleasures that I was loathe to give up — a kind of elitist spirituality fed by the incomprehension or misunderstanding of outsiders but which would vanish the moment even one other comprehended and understood. I wanted to be in charge of my inner life. I wanted to have the final say-so in my relationship with God.

I had no idea that I had these feelings. I was genuinely surprised at their intensity. I tried the route of theological rationalization: that Christ was my mediator, that the Spirit was praying deeply within me, beyond words, and that a spiritual director would interfere in these primary relationships. But while the theology was sound, the relevance to my condition was not. What I detected in myself was not a fight for theological integrity but a battle with spiritual pride.

It took me exactly one year to ask John to be my spiritual director. But it was not a wasted year. Now I knew at least one of the reasons why the old masters recommended a spiritual director and why they insisted that we never grow out of the need for one. It was because of pride, this incredibly devious, alarmingly insidious evil that is so difficult to detect in myself

172

but so obvious to a discerning friend. At the same time I understood one component of my spiritual loneliness, of not having anyone appreciate the intensity of spiritual struggles and disciplines. Again, pride: pride isolates.

In our first meeting John asked what my expectations were. I didn't have any. I had never done this before and didn't know what to expect. I only knew I wanted to explore the personal dimensions of faith and prayer with a guide instead of working by trial and error as I had been. In reflecting on what has developed in these monthly conversations, three things stand out.

The first thing that I noticed after I began meeting with my spiritual director was a marked increase in spontaneity. Since this person has agreed to pay attention to my spiritual condition with me, I no longer feel solely responsible for watching over it. Now that someone experienced in assessing health and pathology in the life of faith is there to tell me if I am coming off the wall, I quit weighing and evaluating every nuance of attitude and behavior. I have always had a tendency to compulsiveness in spiritual disciplines and would often persist in certain practices whether I felt like it or not, year in and year out, in a stubborn determination to provide the conditions in which I would be ready and receptive for whatever the Spirit had for me. I knew the dangers of obsessive rigidity and tried to guard against it. But that was just the problem. I was the disciplinarian of my inner life, the one being disciplined, and the supervisor of my disciplinarian — a lot of roles to be shifting in and out of through the day. I immediately gave up being "supervisor" and shared "disciplinarian" with my director. The psychic load was reduced markedly. I relaxed. I was no longer afraid that if I diverged from my rule I would be subject to creeping self-indulgence, quite sure it would be spotted in short order by my director. I trusted my intuitions more, knowing that self-deceit would be called to account sooner or later by my director. The line that divided my structured times of prayer and meditation from the rest of my life blurred. I no longer had the entire responsibility for deciding how to shape the disciplines. I found myself more spontaneous, more free to innovate, more at ease in being nonproductive and playful.

Another thing that I became aware of is that there are subject matters that I rarely, if ever, talk about with other people in my life that I regularly bring to my director. These are not shameful things that I want to keep hidden, nor are they flattering things about which I am reticent to speak out of modesty. They are the mundane, ordinary things in my life. I don't bring them up in everyday conversation because I don't want to bore my family and friends. I don't want people to lose interest in me and look for a more exciting conversationalist in the same way that they have gone looking for a better banjo player. But these matters take up a great deal of my life. By expressing interest in who I *am* (not what I do) and directing attention to what *is* (not what ought to be or what I want things to be), my director makes conversational reflection possible in these areas.

I am used to looking for the signs of God's presence in crisis and in blessing. I am forced to look to God when I have failed or sinned. I am already motivated to look to God when everything comes together in an experience of wholeness and arrival. But the random ordinary? That is when I am getting ready for the next triumph. Or drifting into the next disaster. But how about exploring that everyday ordinariness for the presence of God and the workings of grace? When "nothing is going on," is there, perhaps, something going on? The flat times, the in-between times, the routine behaviors are also (in the words of Gerard Manley Hopkins) "charged with the grandeur of God." I have always known that but have been fitful

174

and sporadic in exploring the territory. Now, because there is this person with whom I don't have to hold up my end of the conversation, I have space and leisure to take expeditions into the ordinary. I remembered James Joyce's insistence that "literature deals with the ordinary; the unusual and extraordinary belong to journalism,"[4] and saw the analogy to what was going on in these conversations. I think that if a really large problem loomed in my life right now I would be reluctant to talk it over with my director because it would take time away from attending to this larger world of the unproblematic.

A third thing that has struck me is the difference in being in touch with an oral tradition as compared to a written one. I discovered the prayer masters of the church at an early age and subsequently immersed myself in their writings. Their experience and analysis are familiar to me. I profit from reading them. Some of them seem very alive and contemporary. For a long time that seemed to suffice. But there is a radical difference between a book and a person. A book that tells me about the dark night and the person who comments on *my* dark night, even though the words are the same, are different. I can read with detachment; I cannot listen with detachment. The immediacy and intimacy of conversation turn knowledge into wisdom.

There is also the matter of timing. Out of the scores of writers on prayer, the hundreds of truths about faith, and the myriad penetrating truths of the spiritual life, which one is appropriate right now? Searching through indexes to find the page where a certain subject is presented is not the same as having a person notice and name the truth that I am grappling with right now in my own life.

---

4. James Joyce, quoted by William Barrett, *Time of Need* (New York: Harper & Row, 1972), p. 140.

In meetings with my spiritual director, I have often had the sense of being drawn into a living, oral tradition. I am in touch with a pool of wisdom and insight in the life of faith and the practice of prayer in a way different from when I am alone in my study. It is not unlike the experience I have in worship as I participate in Scripture readings, preaching, hymn-singing, and sacraments. These are not so much subjects that you know *about* as an organic life that you enter *into*. In spiritual direction I am guided to attend to my uniqueness in the large context and discern more precisely where my faith development fits on the horizon of judgment and grace.

∴∴∴

Quite obviously none of these experiences depends on having a spiritual director. None of them was new to me in kind but only in degree. Some people develop marvelously in these areas without ever having so much as heard of a spiritual director. Still, for most of the history of the Christian faith it was expected that a person should have a spiritual director. In some parts of the church it is expected still. It is not an exceptional practice. It is not for those who are gifted in prayer or more highly motivated than the rest. In fact, as responsibility and maturity increase in the life of faith the subtleties of temptation also increase and the urgency of having a spiritual director increases.

Søren Kierkegaard wrote in his *Concluding Unscientific Post-script* that spiritual direction "must explore every path, must know where the errors lurk, where the moods have their hiding places, how the passions understand themselves in solitude (and every man who has passion is always to some degree solitary, it is only the slobberers who wear their hearts wholly on their sleeves); it must know where the illusions spread their

176

temptations, where the bypaths slink away."[5] The greatest errors in the spiritual life are not committed by the novices but by the adepts. The greatest capacity for self-deceit in prayer comes not in the early years but in the middle and late years. It strikes me that it is not wise to treat lightly or as a matter of personal taste what most of the generations of Christians have agreed is essential.

---

5. Søren Kierkegaard, *Concluding Unscientific Postscript* (Princeton: Princeton University Press, 1941), pp. 382-83.

IX

Practicing Spiritual Direction

FIVE PASTORS had a turn at providing spiritual direction for George Fox in the first months of his religious awakening. Each of them failed badly. Fox was in his late adolescence when he ran into this discouraging sequence of spiritual misdirections. He does not identify the nature of the trouble that prompted him to seek out the pastors. Sometimes he refers to it as "despair and temptation." It is clear, though, that he was seeking for God. And not one of the five pastors noticed.

That the five did badly is not surprising. George Fox was complex. Spiritual direction is difficult. Pastoral wisdom is not available on prescription. Every person who comes to a pastor with a heart full of shapeless longings and a head full of badgering questions is complex in a new way. There are no fail-proof formulae.

Fox tells the story in his *Journal*. By reflecting on these unsuitable but representative responses from pastoral colleagues of three hundred years past we learn at least how *not* to do it. Only the pastors who are ignorant of history are condemned to repeat it.

First Pastor: Nathaniel Stephens

After some time I went into my own country again, and was there about a year, in great sorrows and troubles, and walked many nights by myself. Then the priest of Drayton, the town of my birth, whose name was Nathaniel Stephens, came often to me, and I went often to him; and another priest sometimes came with him; and they would give place to me to hear me, and I would ask them questions, and reason with them. And this priest Stephens asked me a question, viz, "why Christ cried out upon the cross, 'My God, my God, why hast thou forsaken me?' and why He said, 'If it be possible let this cup pass from me; yet not my will, but thine be done.'" I told him that at that time the sins of all mankind were upon Him, and their iniquities and transgressions with which He was wounded, which He was to bear, and to be an offering for them as He was man, but died not as He was God; and so, in that He died for all men, and tasted death for every man, He was an offering for the sins of the whole world. This I spake, being at that time in a measure sensible of Christ's sufferings, and what He went through. And the priest said it was a very good, full answer, and such a one as he had not heard. At that time he would applaud and speak highly of me to others; and what I said in discourse to him on the week-days he would preach of on the First-days, for which I did not like him. This priest afterwards became my great persecutor.[1]

Nathaniel Stephens turns the conversation of spiritual direction into theological inquiry. He talks like an intellectual dilettante, collecting opinions and savoring nuances of flavor ("the priest said it was a very good, full answer, and such a one as he had

---

1. George Fox, *Journal* (London: J. M. Dent & Sons, 1924), p. 4.

not heard"). The conversations were no doubt stimulating. Neither Stephens nor Fox would have spent so much time talking if they had not found the exchanges interesting. But regardless of the seriousness of the subject matter — God, the soul, temptation — the conversations themselves were not serious. Dialogue degenerated into chatter.

Stephens gives his dilettante game away when he preaches on Sundays the material he gathers from Fox on weekdays. Fox was his theological bin of illustrations. This inquirer, brimming with insights, is plundered for the purpose of sermonizing. Did it never occur to Stephens to ask himself or Fox why the questions were important or what difference they made in their actual living? Apparently not. He does not deal with dignity and respect toward the person (himself as well as Fox) asking questions and seeking answers of God.

The attraction of Stephens's approach for pastors is enormous. Everyone who comes for help is a fascinating case study in living theology in the shape of this woman, the profile of this man. We shift our attention from book to person easily enough, but no corresponding shift takes place in *us* — we "read" the person as impersonally as we read the book. The effect is disastrous. To treat anyone as a theological butterfly, no matter how much care we convey in pinning them to the mounting board and studying the markings of identification, is a violation. If we reduce a person to sermon material, we are agents of alienation.

This theological/intellectual relationship was not without attraction for Fox ("I went often to him"), but it finally failed. Can I remember this? If this person who had dared to begin to think with personal passion about God realizes that I see our encounters as only a theological diversion from the humdrum of duller parishioners (and a source of preaching material), his disillusionment is certain. When a person comes to

181

me for spiritual direction it is not to get into a theological discussion but to find a friend in a theological context.

Second Pastor: "Ancient Priest at Mancetter"

After this I went to another ancient priest at Mancetter, in Warwickshire, and reasoned with him about the ground of despair and temptations; but he was ignorant of my condition; he bade me take tobacco and sing psalms. Tobacco was a thing I did not love, and psalms I was not in a state to sing; I could not sing. Then he bade me come again, and he would tell me many things; but when I came again he was angry and pettish, for my former words had displeased him. He told my troubles, and sorrows, and griefs to his servants so that it was got among the milk-lasses, which grieved me that I had opened my mind to such a one. I saw they were all miserable comforters; and this brought my troubles more upon me.[2]

The ancient priest at Mancetter is a clerk in an ecclesiastical drugstore. He has a stock of folk wisdom that he mixes with churchly admonition and then dispenses like an apothecary. He probably thought of himself as a font of cracker-barrel remedies respected in the community for his common sense. The combination "tobacco and psalms" does give that impression.

The problem was not only in his advice but also in the intent with which he gave it. He reveals his motives when he gets angry at Fox's refusal to buy. Fox, a stubborn customer, refuses the prescribed medicine. That constitutes a rejection for the priest. If Fox won't "take tobacco and sing psalms," then

---

2. Ibid., pp. 4-5.

the salesman has lost a customer. His anger is the appropriate, if tactless, response.

The priest doesn't see Fox as a person to be directed but as a consumer of spiritual goods, a possible buyer of a remedy. A relationship is ventured on the potential buyer's acceptance of the priest's commodities. Rejection dissolves the relationship. When the gossip got around to the milkmaids, Fox realized that the priest did not care about him at all but only whether he took the advice. After Fox refused the advice, not liking tobacco and not able to sing psalms, he knew by the priest's anger that he had been depersonalized into a customer — and a bad customer at that. Since Fox rejected the advice, the priest rejected Fox, refusing to tolerate such unresponsive material in his store. Best get rid of him by deriding him.

Dismissal by derision is part of the syndrome. If a parishioner will not follow our advice he or she is aggravating evidence of our incompetence. The easiest way out is to hint among the milkmaids that there are matters of concern here about stability, immaturity, or neurosis.

Third Pastor: "Priest Living about Tamworth"

Then I heard of a priest living about Tamworth, who was accounted an experienced man, and I went seven miles to him; but I found him like an empty hollow cask.[3]

The daily difficulty for pastors in the work of spiritual direction is the insufficiency of technique, skill, and reputation. These can carry us through many a routine, but when a genuinely troubled person shows up, wrestling with the angels, grappling

---

3. Ibid., p. 5.

with the demons, our *souls* are on the line, tested in the desert. If we are unprepared to engage in honest, open, shared inquiry after God, then we are of no use: "an empty hollow cask."

These inquiries are always an implied threat, for we never know when their relentless searching will expose some undetected shallowness, some unexamined platitude in us. We devise stratagems and roles that allow us to function smoothly and successfully, without pain, anguish, and undue expenditure of psychic energy. But none of this can be sustained in an acutely personal spiritual encounter.

A faddish interest in pastoral counseling is sometimes (not always) a role — the acquisition of a new technique at the expense of becoming a new person. A rigorous discipline aimed at excellence in the pulpit is sometimes (not always) a role — public performance that avoids the pain of praying with people. Instead of giving ourselves into an integration of person and pastor, we learn techniques that give a facade of expertise in spirituality and a reputation for caring. But it only takes a single George Fox to perforate the role-image.

Reputations do not count in spiritual direction. "Experience" is not enough in the pastor's study. When George Fox walks in it is a new ball game. The stories we trot out to illustrate an experience, the insights we use to illuminate personality development, however impressive, will not survive the restless probing of a troubled soul. Only a life committed to spiritual adventure, personal integrity, honest and alert searching prayer is adequate for the task. Fox will spot the "empty hollow cask" every time even if "accounted an experienced man."

Thus, our primary task is to be a pilgrim. Our best preparation for the work of spiritual direction is an honest life. Prayer and the developing capacity for adoration and joy authenticate pastoral existence.

184

Fourth Pastor: Dr. Cradock

I heard also of one called Dr. Cradock of Coventry, and went to him. I asked him the ground of temptations and despair, and how troubles came to be wrought in man. He asked me, "Who was Christ's father and mother?" I told him, "Mary was his mother, and that He was supposed to be the son of Joseph, but He was the Son of God." Now, as we were walking together in his garden, the alley being narrow, I chanced, in turning, to set my foot on the side of a bed, at which the man was in such a rage as if his house had been on fire. Thus all our discourse was lost, and I went away in sorrow, worse than I was when I came. I thought them miserable comforters, and saw they were all as nothing to me; for they could not reach my condition.[4]

Dr. Cradock is concerned about orthodoxy, not only theologically but peripatetically. His concern is that Fox think straight thoughts and walk a straight path. His anger when Fox stepped off the path into his flower bed was not an unfortunate lapse but a telltale expression of his mentality. In Dr. Cradock's mind, deviation from the straight and narrow causes that which is wrong with the world. For him, human despair is rooted in wrong thinking. Fix a person's theology and you will fix him. A dogmatician, Cradock's response to a despairing inquirer is to ask the testing question. He operated as an examining professor, searching out what was wrong with Fox's belief structure. When he found it, he would be able to instruct him in what to believe so that he would be whole again. He had only to find out how Fox diverged from the model of orthodox Christianity in order to set him straight.

---

4. Ibid.

Dr. Cradock's progeny in the twentieth century are as likely to have psychological presuppositions as theological. Freud has preempted Calvin as the father of orthodoxy among many pastors. Today's question has changed from "Who was Christ's father and mother?" to "What do you think of your mother?" — but with the same intent: to get material for diagnosis, data to compare with the orthodox model.

Fortunately, Fox did not have to endure the inquisition very long — Cradock showed his hand, flaring in anger over the garden trespass. Fox, an impossible candidate for any procrustean bed, sorrowfully went looking for other help.

Orthodoxy cannot be imposed. The spiritual director is in an enviable place to observe the endless variations of grace, the fantastic fertility of the divine Spirit bringing faith into creation. But "we can never know just how Christ will be formed in another."[5] If we should mistakenly do our work in the dogmatic schoolmaster style of Dr. Cradock, we well deserve the epitaph "miserable comforter."

Fifth Pastor: "One Macham"

After this, I went to another, one Macham, a priest in high account. He would needs give me some physic, and I was to have been let blood; but they could not get one drop of blood from me, either in arms or heart (though they endeavored it), my body being, as it were, dried up with sorrow, grief and troubles, which were so great upon me that I could have wished I had never been born, or that I had been born blind, that I might never have seen vanity and wickedness, and deaf, that

---

5. Dietrich Bonhoeffer, *Life Together* (New York: Harper & Brothers, 1954).

I might never have heard vain and wicked words, or the Lord's name be blasphemed.[6]

Macham is an activist. He will not waste time with idle talk or useless listening. Something has to be *done*. No matter what, *do* something: "Give him a physic and take some blood."

The suggestion to *do* something is nearly always inappropriate, for persons who come for spiritual direction are troubled over some disorder or dissatisfaction in *being*, not *doing*. They need a friend who will pay attention to who they are, not a project manager who will order additional busywork. Precipitate actions are usually avoidances. They distract for the time being and provide temporary (and welcome) relief. The attraction for "giving a physic and letting blood" is nearly irresistible in a highly ambiguous situation. The sense of definition provided by clearcut action provides tremendous satisfaction. But there is no growth in the spirit, no development into maturity.

Pastors are particularly imperiled in this area because of the compulsive activism, both cultural and ecclesiastical, in which we are immersed simply by being alive at this time in history. It takes wary and persistent watching to avoid falling into the activist trap.

George Fox needed a pastor who was secure enough to absorb, reflect, and tolerate the ambiguity of his troubled despair and temptation and strong enough *not* to have done something to or for him. That would have provided space for the Holy Spirit to initiate the new life. *That* might have made a difference.

∴∴

---

6. Fox, *Journal,* p. 5.

Is there anything that I can do to avoid perpetuating the malpractice of George Fox's five pastors? Are there ways to prepare myself for the next George Fox who waits after a meeting until everyone has gone and ventures a shy question? Or catches me on the street and asks if she can have a few minutes over coffee? Or writes a letter? Or, more deliberately and formally, arranges for a series of conversations to "get at what's bothering me"? A pastor, says Richard Baxter, must not "slightly slubber over" this work.[7] The negatives of Fox's experience suggest some positives.

For a start, I can cultivate an attitude of awe. I must be prepared to marvel. This face before me, its loveliness scored with stress, is in the image of God. This fidgety and slouching body that I am looking at is a temple of the Holy Ghost. This awkward, slightly asymmetrical assemblage of legs and arms, ears and mouth, is part of the body of Christ. Am I ready to be amazed at what God hath wrought, or am I industriously absorbed in pigeon-holing my observations? Is what I see enhanced by faith-instructed imagination or reduced to what can be sorted out and fit into the file-folders of biology and psychology and sociology? Why is it that the minute a person sits down in front of me whose face is an unconvincing image of God, or whose body is a parody of the Holy Ghost's temple, or whose words and actions show no evident coordination with the limbs and organs of Christ's body, I so quickly abandon my basic orientation and the texts that I have pondered and preached and taught for all these years and take up with half-digested slogans and formulae that I pick out of the air of contemporania?

My basic orientation as a pastor is that the significance of

---

7. Richard Baxter, *The Reformed Pastor,* ed. Hugh Martin (Richmond: John Knox Press, 1956), p. 119.

what I see before me is not what I see before me but what Christ has said and done. Far more relevant than what I feel or think, or what this person feels or thinks, is what Christ has said and done. This is a person for whom Christ died, a person he loves: an awesome fact! This is a person preserved alive until this very moment in a world of hurtling automobiles, ravaging diseases, and psychotic menaces. Am I prepared to admire? Am I prepared to respect? Am I prepared to be in reverence?

When I am cast in the role of spiritual authority, only an incessant vigilance prevents me from responding with condescending paternalism. If they are going to look up to me, how can I keep from looking down on them? Not in contempt, to be sure, but in a kind of I-understand-what-is-best-for-you reductionism. But when I do that they leave the conversation benignly belittled.

For many years now I have paid special attention to pastors when they talk about the people they baptize and to whom they give the word and body and blood of Christ. What do they *really* think of them? How rarely do I hear any awe or marvel in their speech, how seldom detect any applause for the glories no one else notices, the grace everyone overlooked. George Fox was a remarkable person, but not one of his five pastors had the faintest inkling of it.

Every meeting with another person is a privilege. In pastoral conversation I have chances that many never get as easily or as frequently — chances to spy out suppressed glory, ignored blessing, forgotten grace. I had better not miss them.

Second, I can cultivate an awareness of my ignorance. There is so much about this person that I don't know. There are layered years of experience that I have no access to. There are feelings of anger and joy and faith and despair that will never be articulated. There are dreams and fantasies of vanity and accomplishment, sexuality and adventure, that will never

see the light of day. Bits and pieces will be hinted at in conversation, but most of it will remain uncharted territory. One
gets the impression that George Fox's five pastors had him
figured out, and God's will for him figured out, in about the
first ten or fifteen minutes.

It is difficult to retain an awareness of my ignorance.
Pastors have passed so many examinations, heard so many
lectures, read so many books, and have so much experience in
the raw material of truth — death, grief, suffering, celebration,
guilt, love — that we easily assume a posture of all-knowing.
But there is so much more that we don't know. We are barely
across the threshold of comprehension. "In no other century
of our brief existence," writes Lewis Thomas, "have human
beings learned so deeply, and so painfully, the extent and depth
of their ignorance."[8] All the same, it is hard not to be impressed
with what I *do* know. I have read and studied the Scriptures
for years and am ambitious to share what I have learned. I have
been taught and trained in theology for years and am eager to
pass on what I know. Given the stimulus of a question or the
signal of a search, I spill out answers and commentary. I want
to get the fullness in my head into the emptiness in the other
head. But what if it is not heads that are involved here but
something more like hearts, *lives?* There is far more, then, that
I don't know than I do know. "It is the mark of an uneducated
mind," says von Hugel, "to be more dogmatic than the subject
allows." I had better be quiet for a while, and listen and watch.
There is more here than meets the eye. There is a lot that hasn't
been said. What is it?

An even more sobering dimension to my ignorance re-
gards God. What has God been doing with this person before

---

8. Lewis Thomas, *The Medusa and the Snail* (New York: Viking Press,
1979), p. 16.

he or she showed up in my study? What messages have been received, distorted, missed? God has been at work with this person since birth. Everything that has taken place in this life has in some way or another taken place in the context of a good creation and an intended salvation. Everything.

When this person leaves my presence the good creation and the intended salvation will remain basic. God's grace is in operation and will persist. My words and gestures and actions take place in the midst of a great drama, about the details of which I know little or nothing. In no way does that mean that my part is unimportant or dispensable. I take with absolute seriousness whatever part I play, but I am a supporting player and not the lead. I do my very best, but in no way do I speak or act so that the person's response to *me* is the center-stage action. God wants to meet with this person; this person wants, unfocused as the want may be, to meet with God. I must not manipulate the conversation or construe the setting so that I am perceived to be in charge, or I merely delay the things of God.

Third, I can cultivate a predisposition to prayer. My undergirding assumption in all pastoral encounters is that what the person really wants from me is to learn how to pray or to be guided to maturity in prayer. That assumption is not always confirmed by later developments, but less is lost in making the assumption wrongly than in mistakenly not making it.

It is easier to talk about ideas or people or projects. For the moment that is usually satisfying enough. But if it is God with whom the person really wants to deal, all I have done is divert the search or delay the meeting. I have mistaken myself as the primary partner in the conversation when what the person is really looking for is conversation with God. If I dominate the conversation, either ignoring God's word and presence and mercy or consigning him to a merely ceremonial position, then I am getting in the way.

191

It is God with whom we have to do. People go for long stretches of time without being aware of that, thinking that it is money, or sex, or work, or children, or parents, or a political cause, or an athletic competition, or learning with which they must deal. Any one or a combination of these subjects can absorb them and for a time give them the meaning and purpose that human beings seem to require. But then there is a slow stretch of boredom. Or a disaster. Or a sudden collapse of meaning. They want more. They want God. When a person searches for meaning and direction, asking questions and testing out statements, we must not be diverted into anything other or lesser.

This does not mean that the pastor's task is to get people on their knees with the least possible delay. It doesn't mean that we have an instruction manual on prayer in which we assign lessons. Many times there will be no formal or verbalized prayer. Often there will be no explicit reference to prayer. But there must be a predisposition toward prayer, a readiness for prayer. Spiritual direction is then conducted with an awareness that it takes place in God's active presence, and that our conversation is therefore conditioned by his speaking and listening, his *being there*.

This cannot be reduced to procedure or formula. It is not accomplished so much by what we do or say to another but in the way we *are* when we meet another. Clement of Alexandria called prayer "keeping company with God." "Keeping company" involves gesture and silence, relaxed musing and intent saying. Other persons can join and leave the company without disrupting it. More often than we think, the unspoken, sometimes unconscious reason that persons seek out conversation with the pastor is a desire to keep company with God; if they are unlucky enough to come to a pastor who is not active in the company, they are going to be disappointed as George Fox was, none of whose pastors gave any direction in prayer or was perceived to be a person of prayer.